THE
BOOK
☙ OF ☙
KEYS

Authored and referenced by
A Man who Seeks That which Is Above
Zachary Ziolkowski

ISBN 978-1-0980-0775-1 (paperback)
ISBN 978-1-0980-0918-2 (hardcover)
ISBN 978-1-0980-0776-8 (digital)

Christian Faith Publishing, Inc.
832 Park Avenue
Meadville, PA 16335
www.christianfaithpublishing.com

Printed in the United States of America

INTRODUCTION

I beseech you therefore, brethren, by the mercies of God, that ye present your bodies a living sacrifice, holy, acceptable unto God, which is your reasonable service. And be not conformed to this world: but be ye transformed by the renewing of your mind, that ye may prove what is that good, and acceptable, and perfect, will of God. (Romans 12:1–2)

For I say unto you, That except your righteousness shall exceed the righteousness of the scribes and Pharisees, ye shall in no case enter into the kingdom of heaven. (Matthew 5:20)

But it is the spirit in a person, the breath of the Almighty, that gives them understanding. (Job 32:8)

For the prophecy came not in old time by the will of man: but holy men of God spake as they were moved by the Holy Ghost. (2Peter 1:21)

For whatsoever things were written aforetime were written for our learning, that we through patience and comfort of the scriptures might have hope. (Romans 15:4)

But continue thou in the things which thou hast learned and hast been assured of, knowing of whom thou hast learned them; and that from a child thou hast known the holy scriptures, which are able to make thee wise unto salvation through faith which is in Christ Jesus. All scripture is given by inspiration of God, and is profitable for doctrine, for reproof, for correction, for instruction in righteousness: that a man of God may be perfect, throughly furnished unto all good works. (2Timothy 3:14–17)

Yea, a man may say, thou hast faith, and I have works: shew me your faith without thy works, and I will shew thee my faith by my works. (James 2:18)

For we must appear before the judgment seat of Christ: that every one may receive the things done in his body, according to that he hath done, whether it be good or bad. (2Corinthians 5:10)

For all have sinned, and come short of the glory of God; Being justified freely by his grace through the redemption that is in Christ Jesus: (Romans 3:23–24)

For whosoever shall call upon the name of the Lord shall be saved. (Romans 10:13)

And from Jesus Christ, who is the faithful witness, and the first begotten of the dead, and the prince of the kings of the earth. Unto him that loved us, and washed us from our sins in his own blood, And hath made us kings and priests unto God and his Father; to him be glory and dominion for ever and ever. Amen. (Revelation 1:5–6)

If ye then, being evil, know how to give good gifts unto you child, how much more shall your Father which is in heaven give good thing to them that ask him? Therefor all things whatsoever ye would that men should do to you, do ye even to them: for this is the law and the prophets. Enter ye in a straight gate: for wide is the gate, and broad is the way, that leadth to destruction, and many there be which go in therat: Because strait is the gate, and narrow is the way, which leadth unto life, and few there be that find it. Beware of false prophets, which come to you in sheep's clothing, but inwardly they are ravening wolves. Ye shall know them by their fruits. Do men gather grapes of thorns, or figs of thistles? (Matthew 7:11–16)

Not every one that saith unto me Lord, Lord, shall enter into the kingdom of heaven: but he that doeth the will of my Father which is in heaven. Many will say to me in that day, Lord, Lord, have we not prophesied in thy name? and in thy name have cast out devils? And in thy name done many wonderful works? And then I will profess unto them, I never knew you: depart from me, ye that work iniquity. (Matthew 7:21–23)

Remember therefor from whence thou art fallen, and repent, and do the first works; or else I will come unto thee quickly, and will remove thy candlestick out of his place, except thou repent. (Revelation 2:5)

For God so loved the world, that He gave His only begotten Son, that whoever believes in Him shall not perish but have everlasting life. (John 3:16)

Herein is our love made perfect, that we may have boldness in the day of judgment: because as he is, so are we in this world. There is no fear in love; but perfect love casteh out fear: because fear hath torment. He that fearth is not made perfect in love. We love him, because he first loved us. (1 John 4:17–19)

CONTENTS

CHAPTER 1

—⚜—

KEY OF TRUTH

The first key I will write about is the key of truth, and let me start off with a quote from Jesus. "I am the way and the truth and the life. No one comes to the father except through me" (John 14:6).

Yes, this is a Christian book, but anyone can read it. Every parent will carry this key, but it is not a key for them. It is a key for their child, and it will define the very foundation of their child's life. A child's mind is inexperienced with all things concerning them, and they are completely free of consequence. That is why they will ask their parents the most important question everyone will ask at some point in their life. *Why!* And it's usually followed by the second and third most important questions. *Why!!!* Get the picture yet?

Now, a smart man or woman can usually satisfy why a few times, but eventually, the child will outsmart the adult because of the power of that simple word. When I was a boy, I had to know everything, how it worked, and I am still like that. I asked my father, "Why is the sky blue?"

He said, "It was because of the gases and the light that reflected off of them." Now, mind you, I was very young at this point.

I again questioned him by saying, "Why does the light shine through the gases and make the sky blue?" How would you answer this question? You can take any question you could ever ask and ask why again and again and it will lead you to this crossroad at which point; you will have a choice to make. Do you tell or believe the truth or do you tell or believe a lie to satisfy a young mind.

My father told the truth, and this is what he said "I don't know. God made it that way for a reason." And it wasn't just that question he gave that answer for. It was his go to for every question he couldn't answer and I know why. For it is written, "In the beginning God created the heaven and the earth." (Genesis 1:1). "For by him were all things created, that are in heaven, and that are in earth, visible and invisible, whether thrones or dominions or principalities, or powers: all things were created by him, and for him." (Colossians 1:16).

So in his answer, he passed to me the key of truth, which is to say by God were all things created and for His reasons they were created. This is foundation thinking, and the foundation of this thinking is rock solid truth! "Therefore whosoever hearth these saying of mine, and doeth them, I will liken unto a wise man, which build his house upon a rock: And the rain descended, and the floods came, and the winds blew, and beat upon that house: and it fell not: for it was founded upon a rock" (Matthew 7:24–25).

Now let's talk for a minute about the children's foundations that are built on sand. Adolf Hitler was lied to, and worse than that, he believed it. That lie has left a huge mark in mankind's history, and look how it ended for him. His lie of an empire crumbled before the might of united truth. Lying is the greatest weapon of evil because it is the first step in your fall. And it's everyone, including me, that "falls short of the glory of God" (Roman 3:23).

When you tell your child a lie, his life will constantly fall apart. That is why the (true) analogy in the Bible is so true. Your foundation has to be a rock or nothing will stand upright when troubles come your way. My father told me one day, "A lie is easy to defeat because it will not last, but the truth is easy to defend because it cannot be unproven (and also lasts forever)."

Now, I think I know what you're thinking; this guy and his father must be lawyers, and I say, "Ha! I wish." We are both farmers, and even my stepfather is a farmer. Needless to say, I was born and destined to be a farmer, but I'll get to why that is in a later chapter.

Parents, you really need to be careful with this key, not only for your child's sake, but yours as well. There's a saying somewhere out there, "If you lie long enough, loud enough, and often" (oops its) "If you live long enough, you'll watch yourself become your own worst enemy (Thanks, Batman)," or something like that. That's because we are a hardheaded people. We want things set in stone, our way, in our selfishness. God is selfless and the only one I know of that has set in stone—things that were, are, and will be. And if I'm not mistaken, He used His finger and His word alone. If it's too late, I assure you it's never too late. If you weren't able to set the foundation of thinking in your child, don't worry. We still have a planet of Christians working for God; and by God you pray for your child and "God will send a comforter your way" (John 14:16). This is the "Key of Truth."

CHAPTER 2

— ❧ —

KEY OF LAWS

Now that I've certainly convinced you that God is the real deal—just kidding, of course—but I will certainly keep trying to convince you by imparting a little knowledge regarding God's laws. I will first start by stating that the commandments are to be kept! Otherwise (Genesis 26:5) (Exodus 20:6. Do I really have to give you a reference from this book of laws?) (Leviticus 18:26; 19:19; 19:37; 20:8; 20:22; 22:31; 25:18; 26:3) (Numbers 15:40) (Deuteronomy 4:1; 4:5; 4:6; 4:14; 4:40; 5:1; 5:29; 6:1–2; 6:17; 6:24; 7:11; 8:1; 8:6; 10:13; 11:1; 11–8; 11:32; 13:4; 13:18; 15:5; 16:12; 17:19; 26:16; 27:10; 28:9; 28:13; 28:58; 29:29; 30:8; 30:10; 30:16; 31:12; 32:46) (Joshua 22:5; 23:6) (Judges 2:17) (All of Ruth! Summed up best in the reapers responses in Ruth 2:11–13; 3:11) (1 Samuel 15:1) (2 Samuel 22:23) (1 Kings 2:3; 6:12; 8:61; 9:4; 11:38) (2 Kings 17:13; 17:37; 21:8) (1 Chronicles 29:18–19) (2 Chronicles 30:12) (Ezra 10:1–5) (Nehemiah 1:9) (Esther 1:11–13) (Job 1:1,5) (Psalm 78:7; 105:45 119:2; 119:4) (Proverbs 7:2–4) (Ecclesiastes 12:13).

Song of Solomon is a hard one to get. I believe that book is quite possibly the most misunderstood book in the Bible. I think the author(s) were trying to explain what love truly is in this poem. As in the love God made. When it comes to the keeping of the commandments though, look at the charges against the women of Jerusalem. "I charge you, O ye daughters of Jerusalem, by the roes, and by the hinds of the field, that ye stir not up, nor awake my love, till he please" (Song of Solomon 2:7).

I don't think that's referring to Solomon getting his beauty sleep. It's more like it's saying the women of Jerusalem are doing something to stir up and or awaken God through displeasing him; "therefore do not do," as it states. And you can only charge someone if they break a law or you bear false witness (False witness was a big deal and punishable by death). I'll close this book and let you get back to referencing after these last verses. I will first write the verses and then write it out with editing notes which my heart, through God's spirit, has shown me. Song of Solomon 8:4–14.

> I come against you, O daughters of Jerusalem, that ye not be unlawful, nor awake God, until his appointed time. God cometh up from the wilderness, leaning upon her beloved. He raised thee up by the Word of the LORD under the apple tree: there thy mother brought thee forth: there she brought thee forth that bares Gods Word. Set me as the commands upon thine heart, as works done with thine arm: for love is as strong (unbreakable, unchanging, but most of all is as certain as) as death; sin is as cruel as eternal death: which the works there are the works of evil, which hath a most intense ending. Many works cannot quench God from having to have to punish us; neither can the people take Him away: if a man would give away all his earthly possessions for the pursuit of God, he would absolutely be hated for it.

Forgive me if editing this has offended thee, but I did it not out of hate nor am I attempting to make this a private interpretation (2 Peter 1:20). I want you to see what my heart is thinking. This book has been a joy to go through (like twenty times). I hope you have taken pause to consider these things I speak of. Going through all these references would be a little boring without a stir of thoughts. (Isaiah 1:19, 56:4) (Jeremiah 7:23) (Lamentations is exactly what happens when you don't keep the law)(Ezekiel 11:20, 20:19, 36:27, 44:24) (Daniel 9:4, and he was thrown in the lions' den for loving God)(Hosea 2:12–13, 6:5–7, 8:12–13) (Joel 2:11–14) (Amos 2:4) (Obadiah 1:3–18) (Jonah 3:10, and also his job was to deliver God's word to Nineveh) (Micah 6:8) (Nahum 1:15) (Habakkuk 1:1–5) (Zephaniah 1:17–2:3) (Haggai 1:5–7) (Zechariah 3:7) (Malachi 2:1–4) (Matthew 19:17–19) (Mark 7:7–10) (Luke 11:28) (John 14:15, 15:10) (Acts 15:5, 21:24) (Romans 7:12) (1Corinthians 7:19) (2 Corinthians 3) (Galatians 3:10, 5:14) (Ephesians 2:14–16, 5:1–10) (Philippians 1:10, 2:3, 2:12–16) (Colossians 2:18–22, 3:15) (1 Thessalonians 1:3, 5:15–24) (2 Thessalonians 2:14–17, 3:5–6) (1 Timothy 6:14) (2 Timothy 2:5, 2:13–16) (Titus 1:12–16, 3:8) (Philemon 1:10–21. If you have trouble with this one, it's a metaphor of Jesus. The law was unprofitable until Jesus came and made it profitable through Him.) (Hebrews 2:1–4, 3:7–13, 4:1–12, 5:12–14, 6:1–7, 6:10–11, all of Chapter 8, 10:16–17, 10:36. Just read chapter 11, I can't reference one verse alone—it's too great) (James 1:22) (1Peter 2:15, 4:8) (2 Peter 2:21, 3:1–9) (1 John 5:3) (2 John 1:6) (3 John 1:8–11) (Jude 1:21) (Revelation 12:17, 14:12–13) (otherwise) all these are just a load of crap, and I should stop writing this book of keys here and now. But no, I say; this is how important this topic is. This took me a month of Sundays to compile this list of references. And even more time that I could confirm and understand them. And those are just the ones I found. And if you have made it through all these yourself you too shall understand we are to keep the law. Besides I don't know how to unwrite something wrote on the heart and the mind! (Jeremiah 31:33, Hebrews 10:16) Now this is a big statement, and I want to separate an argument about works, faith, and works of faith out to a different chapter.

Let's concentrate on the question. Are we to keep the law? This is what I asked, and God answered. It started simple, but very quickly, I saw God's response had expanded to the true nature of what I was asking, which, by the way, is what He does. My question was, "Are we to keep the law?"

His answer was, "Who the law, who not the law, what the law, what not the law, when the law, when not the law, where the law, where not the law, why the law, why not the law, how the law, and how not the law." So it is to say, the true nature of my question was who the law, what the law, when the law, where the law, why the law, and how the law. These questions were preceding the later question. It is *true*; all *answers* will *take you* back *to the beginning*, and *there, you* will always *find God*.

When I was a young boy, my mother was definitely the keeper, upholder, and layer down of the law in our house. God wrote the law in my heart, but Ma upheld it on my butt (with a spatula) (Proverbs 13:24). My ma and dad were divorced at this time, but God was still there with us. She read to me and my brother (who is three years younger than I) the book of Genesis and the book of Exodus. And it just so happened, in the mid-nineties, that there were a couple really good movies about Noah's ark and Moses's exodus. So the books really took in me.

Mothers, I will tell you a secret of life (Sorry, fathers, but still listen up). There is a book, and it is called *Love you forever* by author Robert Munsch, 1986. Read it to your child and observe their eyes. If either of your eyes tear up, you have obtained the secret. Be patient, though. It may take a few tries, but eventually, you'll both figure out what happens to the old sick mother and how it was and will be applicable to your lives (Ecclesiastes 3:2). The secrets of life are to live, to laugh, and to love. That's not just a cheap poster to stick up on the wall—that's the real deal (Not saying I don't have one of those or anything). This was my second foundation thought. Love! (Galatians 5:13–14).

In this chapter of Galatians, it is the willingness to strive to do God's will by obeying/loving His Word. This is what separates the lawful and the unlawful; the willing versus the tolerant. If the Jews were willing to believe in Jesus, they would have believed in Him by their willingness to accept Him, but in their tolerance of Him that only lasted until they couldn't tolerate Him, so they crucified Him. Willingness is truth in spirit, but tolerance is a lie told by your flesh (Galatians 5:16–18). This verse will lead me to my next bit of thoughts. It said, "If the spirit leads you're not under the law." This is because when the spirit leads, it leads as God leads. Righteously!!! It need not know the law because it is a representation of the law. This was really hard to say—that is to say, hard to find the words. I will say it another way. The spirit knows only truth and does only truth, but only the spirit. This is where the flesh cometh in, cause he's like, "I think this is good, but who really cares? It feels good. Let's do it." And that's the flesh!!! The flesh is the true cause of all confusion in the world, and that's why the law was written. It is to define to the flesh what is unlawful (Galatians 3:21–25). Our school master which is to say a good teaching for us to uphold, eventually leading us to Jesus. When we find Jesus, then the spirit begins to lead us, and as I said, when the spirit leads, it knows only truth and does only truth (spoiler alert) which is a true work of faith. A good thought is when in the spirit, don't worry about the law; it knows what it's doing, but when in the flesh, always consider how what you're doing pertains to lawfulness. A person can pop in and out of spirit and flesh because they are contrary one to the other, and we truly are not perfect (Luke chapter 8). We lust after our own self-interests, trying to fulfill ourselves. I was living like this for a long while, but now, this feeling comes and goes. I always get back in spirit by reading the books of the Bible. That is because, truthfully, we long to fulfill the Word of God and receive forgiveness and an open path to Heaven. This gives meaning to our lives.

Now, I will talk shortly about the two most important laws and close on this chapter. The first work (a.k.a. law) is *love God*. This is the beginning. I know I should reference Exodus, but I'm not; I'm gonna reference Deuteronomy 6:5. "You shall love the lord your God with all your heart and with all your soul and with all your might." This is because "For God so loved the world, that he gave his only begotten Son, that whoever believes in him should not perish but have eternal life" (John 3:16). And let's face the truth, "we love him, because he first loved us" (1 John 4:19). I couldn't have it said any better than the Bible can. This world was birthed out of love; that's why God finished every day and creation by saying, "I (God) saw that it was good." Unfortunately, we, male and female, who were made in

God's image (Genesis 1:26) came out of His likeness by breaking the only law that existed at the time. Then, in our law-breaking, it begot more laws and law breaking, and here we sit, thankful God wrote it on our hearts and minds because that would be a never-ending book of laws. The second work (a.k.a. law) is "Love your neighbor as thyself" (Galatians 5:14). Boy if everyone did that we wouldn't need laws. LOL. The "Key of Laws" is this: knowing we will fail, we must strive to uphold God's word, because in our strife are we in the Love of God. (Jude 1:17–25; John 15:10)

CHAPTER 3

—— ✿ ——

KEY OF QUESTIONS

Now that I got the heavy hitters out of the way, let's get to the meat and potatoes of this book. Have you ever wondered why questions exist? There is only one word that can explain questions. That word is *conviction*. The word *conviction* can mean a formal declaration that someone is guilty of an offense and/or a firmly held belief of opinion. So I convict you of wrongdoing, or what is your conviction for why that is? And also, what is your conviction? Your actions weren't unlawful.

Honestly, our human responses are beliefs and opinions, and we surely love to judge everything and make our own opinions rule the roost. This book, however, is about God, so let's get Him in here.

I was arguing with a Christian about DNA one time. He had a book written by a guy, and he was trying to defend what this guy was saying without having put much time and effort into what we were talking about. If you didn't catch that, I was winning the argument, but let me say this; there are no winners of an argument, there is only an opportunity to advance the gospel truth (Philippians 1:12).

He was getting frustrated and made the mistake of saying, "God's is the only opinion that matters." I didn't return a response. I saw that, within the text messages, he was steaming, so I stopped returning texts. (He ended up inviting me to his Baptist church. I go and we are still friends. This is after I said to myself I would never find an assembly in which I can be a part of. Thanks, Cris.)

Think about what he said though, Christians, this is why we need to have the patience of Job (Me too). He said, "God's opinion." This is an oxymoron. What I wanted to say was "God doesn't need to give his opinion—God knows everything" (John 14:2). Any question you can ask, God has an answer to. Search the scriptures (Romans 15:4). I am a man of many questions and have a God of all the answers. God has all the knowledge and understanding there is to know, so if you have questions, ask Him (Proverbs 2:6). Be patient, and He will get back to you. The key is patience; after all, he does have like 8,000,000,000-ish people to serve yearly, monthly, daily, hourly, and on a second-to-second basis.

Now, let's switch gears and talk about questions and that striking word, *conviction*. My fellow brethren of the Baptist religion have three really good questions. Have you been saved? (Romans 10:9–10.) Have you come under the conviction of Jesus? (John 16:8.) If you were standing before God, what would you say? (2 Corinthians 5:10.)

Now, those are really good questions designed to put you under God's conviction, but I am gonna teach you why these questions are doomed to not be as effective as they could be (Out of *love*, brother and sisters. Out of *love*). Deception is a spawn of conviction through the father of lies who is Lucifer? (John 8:44). Look through Revelation. That old serpent deceives all the nations—that includes Christians—and he's very good at it (2 Corinthians 11:14). So with regard to the Baptist questions, the devil has set up in front of your questions in a booth handing out blindfolds so the people cannot see as you see when they get to you. This is hard to understand, so let us look at it another way.

I was talking to my stepfather, Randy, about trapping one day. As in trapping for animal furs. He used to do this when I was a young boy, so I asked him questions regarding the subject. He taught me lots of things regarding things he has done, including farming. He finished by saying, "A master trapper doesn't set his trap ten feet off the road like most people do. He, knowing this, will set his trap all the way upriver to the source of the game if he has to. This will ensure that he will catch the game and yield the fur."

Satan's teachings override those questions because he gets the game. (He doesn't always win though, thankfully. And please do not associate Satan with my stepfather; it just so happened wise trappers are very competitive.) (Mark 4:14–15). So my fellow Baptists and everyone else working for Heaven's sake, go back to the beginning. God teaches our life has meaning and we were created for a reason. Ask someone, "What do you think about God?" The answers will shock you. They will know exactly who and what God is, almost as if it were written into their very DNA (Hebrews 8:11). And if they know and accept him, talk to him or her. You might advance your gospel understandings.

My stepfather also told me, "The day you stop learning how to farm is the day you stop farming." And if they don't accept God, continue talking.

Ask them, "Don't you want to go to heaven?" Now, this is where the conversation gets interesting. So in two questions, I have confirmed their creation by God and confirmed their conviction by God's word. Note that you may have to get creative with the questions everyone is different, but the idea is for them to define God and then put them under God's conviction so they understand they need help like you and I need help. Step two conviction is where the Baptist's questions come in handy, and then from there is all roads to Jesus. He is the help we need. I will prove what I'm saying is true because it is a lot (2 Peter 3:3–18).

Now, this is the exact struggle Christians have. I tried to put him under conviction, but he chose to justify his actions to keep his or her lusts. That's what the greatest liar has set up: self-justification rather than seeking forgiveness for one's own lust. That's where my country went wrong; we traded in forgiveness for tax-funded justification in the 1950s. I will talk more about justification in the next chapter.

A couple sentences back, I said, "From there (conviction) is all roads to Jesus." I will expand on this by saying, "Christianity is a road with infinite paths. The paths being the interpretations, but all roads converge to God's appointed day of judgment, and you better have life's greatest questions answered by then."

When I was in school, we learned about questions. Who? What? When? Where? Why? And sometimes, how? This was the lesson and is also the path every Christian takes in this exact order.

Who is God? Acceptance.

What is heaven? Acceptance.

When is judgment? Depression.

Where am I going after judgment? Bargaining.

Why would I go there? Anger.

How is that possible? Denial.

This will bring us to one accord, and I hate to spoil the surprise, but I'm bent on saving folks for Heaven's sake (Philippians 2:2).

So God is the creator of the heaven and the earth (Genesis 1:1).

Heaven is a place with no evil and filled with wonders you can even imagine (LOL. I can't even imagine a place with no evil) (John 14:2–3; Revelation chapter 20–22).

God will determine the exact time of judgment for his reason (Matthew 24:36).

You're going to heaven or the lake of fire by God's word (There is no option C) (Lake of fire, Revelation 20; Heaven, Revelation 21–22.) Revelation 20:11 says there is no place for them who flee from God.

The life you lived will be justified by the word of God's judgment upon you (Romans 2:6; 2 Corinthians 5:10; 1 Peter 1:17; Revelation 20:12; Psalms 62:12; Proverbs 24:12; 1 Corinthians 3:8; Jeremiah 17:10).

God is how this is possible; he is the first and the last, the alpha and the omega (Revelation 1:8; 21:6–7; 22:13).

And if why alone, don't put the fear of God in you; go back again to the beginning. Why is *thee* the most powerful word? And God's not mean. Let Him, by His Word, tell you why.

So to close this chapter. I say, *everyone question everything* (that comes of man's doing)! (Deuteronomy 13, all of it.) Women, you are included in this; you are taken out of man(Genesis 2:23). And Christians, 1 Peter 3:15.

CHAPTER 4

— ❦ —

KEY OF REASONS

And now for my most hated concept—*justification!* Keep this in mind *always* (Mark 10:18). I truly do hate this concept; however, the only justification I will accept is God's (especially when He doth judge me, that is, assuming He would give me one, and let's face it, I can't contest His judgment; He's God, I'm not). Mankind has run so far out of control with this concept it is not even funny anymore. You could accidently and unintentionally do something to offend someone, and rather than forgiving you when you ask for it, they will say, "Screw you, man," flip you the bird, and call the social justice warriors. That is the future of modern society (which is godless) that we now live in, unfortunately.

Justification is exactly how the Satan got Adam and Eve to believe his lie. Now, let me explain this all, because I want no confusion about this topic. Read these verses, Genesis 3:1–5, a couple of times. Satan's lie was "Ye shall not surely die." Now, this is contrary to what God said (Genesis 2:16–17). The justification is this: "For God doth know that in the day ye eat thereof, then your eyes shall be opened, and ye shall be as gods, knowing good and evil." This justification, as I called it, is a fragment of truth. God says, "And the LORD God said, Behold the man is become as one of us, to know good and evil, and now, lest he put forth his hand, and take also the tree of life, and eat, and live forever" (Genesis 3:22). Then we were taken out of the Garden of Eden. Look at how the second part of what Satan says matches what God says. That was the truth. The lie was to surely die. When a portion of what someone says is not true, no matter how small, *it is a lie*, and justification is the backbone of a lie. If you don't believe what I am saying, the next time someone tells you a lie, ask him why. Remember always the power of that word, because the next thing that comes out of a liar's mouth will be a justifier, which can be true or false. This can be deadly to you, because a good liar will be also a good justifier. Keep asking why, why, why, why, why, why! One of two outcomes will happen. Either he (or she) will storm off, or you will catch them in the lie because it won't last.

Now, I caution you about the true spawns of Satan that are out there lying. They will put their justification in an endless loop. So if your conversation feels like it's going in circles, it's because it is. There is no reasoning with those people; they have chosen the path of endless, absolute hatred. (Genesis 6:5). This is how you catch liars.

Now, let me tell you about the Truth. (Hail, Jesus.) A person who uses truth to defend himself needs no justification, because he has the Word of God defending him (Proverbs 12:19). And I personally would love to see any mere mortal, and even the angels, prove God's Word to be incorrect. (Imagine anyone standing before God telling Him He's wrong—that's a good joke.) That is an impossible act. This is what the truth truly is—an impossible word to break. That is why so much effort is put into corrupting man's understanding of God's Word. God's word cannot be broken, so attack man's understanding of God's Word.

Now, this was a whole lot of reasoning, so let's reason another way. There is a verse in the Bible, and it reads, "But sanctify the Lord God in your hearts: and be ready always to give an answer to every man that asketh you a reason of hope that is in you with meekness and fear" (1 Peter 3:15). This too is a justification and, I guess, the only one I'd be willing to accept from someone.

To hear how God has inspired someone is a wonder and a half. That is good justification which hath stemmed from telling the truth, and in a world of bad justifiers, one can shine a light so bright it will send liars running for the hills (1 John 2:10).

23

I want to take a short pause here after this last sentence to say this: Christianity is an exponential function. My father-in-law would be proud to hear me say that. (He's both a Christian and he was my math teacher.) One talks to two, two to four, and so on and so forth 'til it encompasses the entire earth. That is the power of God's Word which is to encompass mankind (and if you'd like to expedite the process, find a crowd). This is also why the Satans have to work so hard; they must fight the exponential growth to achieve their goals. It is truly unfortunate that the devils kingdom will come, but rest assured that the Kingdom of Christ will come shortly after the devil's crumbles, and God's will last forever (Revelation 11:15 in literally a verse).

So I have witnessed to several people now, and I would like to touch on a phrase I keep running across. It goes like this. "That's not what that means." And to you, I say, "By whose standard?" That usually shuts them up. Not because I am mean about it, but rather, they cannot answer the question. If they do, they condemned their argument. The only two answers are "That's what I think," which is not God's standard, and "That is not what God meant."

To which I then say, "Are we capable of conceiving what God truly meant?" The Christian answer to that should always be no, right? Wrong! As much as I should say no, it would be incorrect to do so. I have come to this understanding, and I will tell you why. I tell people we are capable of understanding, we have minds, and we can interpret just fine. We need not know what God meant, because Him speaking the words that He spoke is more than enough for us to be obedient/loving. So with our minds, we can find reason in God's Word, know this, and know it well. If that reason is incorrect; *it will not hold up to scripture!* That's the built-in failsafe of truth. And if that's not enough for you, consider this: the fear of the LORD is the beginning of knowledge (Proverbs 1:7). The "Key of Reason" is reason. Reason and reason and reason some more, because when reasoning takes you back to the beginning, there, you will find why we come to fear the LORD God. "The fear of the Lord is the beginning of wisdom: and the knowledge of the holy is understanding" (Proverbs 9:10).

CHAPTER 5

——— ❦ ———

KEY OF KNOWLEDGE

I may have written into a wall here having had given away this key in the last chapter, which is to say the "Key of Knowledge" is fear of the LORD, but this is a perfect opportunity to share with you my testimony. So here goes.

When I was boy, as I said, I came to love God because He created everything and for His reasons. I faced the truth and everything I wanted to know, God was the answer. I also received many lessons on being lawful. I, though, at this point, hadn't come to know Jesus and how He worked. I knew His name, I'm sure, but not His purpose. So then came Catholic religion class. I have nothing against any religion—you can believe as you want—I personally believe the Word of God first and foremost; besides, religion isn't the problem. The people are the problem, and that's why Jesus went for the people. And I would like to say this before I continue; our Catholic priest was a good man, a good priest, and a good servant of God. I watched him as a young man stand in front of his congregation asking for forgiveness for taking money. He got scammed, if you're wondering. That thing he did though (asking for forgiveness) has stuck with me for life, and forgiveness is the third and final foundation thought, and I will have a whole chapter dedicated to this.

Back to religion class though. He had no chance. When you're taught you're the descendants of apes, you go planet of the apes. I'm not joking with you; he was a Polish priest, and he actually got so frustrated with our behavior he would swear at us. That's how bad we were. So I still never found Jesus.

So fast forward to 2006, and here is where the story takes a nosedive, literally! I'm going to give you the short of it because I don't like to remember it, though I have put a Valkyrie wing tattoo on my forearm to never forget it. I went to a drinking party, did a shot of Everclear while closing my eyes, somehow got lit on fire, went to the sink, put myself out, passed out from exhaustion, somehow got to the balcony, swan dived off, landed on the concert patio on my face, and somehow survived the flight for life to the burn unit. (If you were there and are reading this book, please keep it to yourself. I know enough not to want to know anymore.)

Let me make sure the picture of this is painted for you. In the police report, the officer stated he would not come to my aid because it was his conviction that I was going to die because of the injuries he could see. There was a girl there that was trying to comfort me as best she could. This was also reported. The flight for life took me to the best burn unit in my state. They, despite my suffering, did an amazing job. They had to wire my jaw shut. I had completely pulverized a small portion of jaw and still have a good deal of hardware left over. It took several surgeries to restore it and also some implants. From the picture I saw, my face and head were the size of an over-inflated balloon. My burns were pretty bad also. The tips of the bottom of my ears, my neck, chest, nipples, right side, front of armpit, elbow, biceps, and forearm were burned. I had to get a couple skin grafts. The worst was my wrist/forearm. It was the arm I used to put myself out. It healed, however, the best of all. I want you to remember the wrist/forearm as this continues. I ate from a feeding tube for a good deal of time, and it was very difficult to convert back to solid food. I also went from 205 pounds down to 150 pounds and just about passed out when I saw that. (I don't recommend this as a dietary course of action; it was exactly as much fun as it sounds.) This is what happened to my flesh. Now let me tell you what happened to my spirit.

Before I say this, I want you to know I don't give a crap what you think about what I am about to say; I lived it, you didn't! (The very definition of testimony.) My spirit or ghost was no longer in the body. I don't know for how long. I was taken to a place, and this is what I saw. Both in third and first person at the same time, I saw myself standing in a pit. The pit was a giant place, yet somehow, I could feel it was enclosed. I couldn't see anyone or anything in there. It was just me, and it was so dark. I have trouble describing the darkness. I felt an overwhelming pressure coming down on me, and it caused my entire being to shake in fear. I can't, in any words, describe to you that feeling of terror. Then, in an instant, an angel of light appeared before me. It did not speak to me; it just stood before me. The light was bright white, so much so that I could not see the features of the being, only the outline. And the outline was this—the outline was of similar shape to a human, but from the bottom of the neck to the top of the hips, wings began and shot out in every direction. There was definitely more than one set of wings, and I felt them without touching them. And I felt this—love. As in the embrace you feel when you are in the arms of the one you love. The feeling was overwhelming *love*.

I must have known somehow, someway, that angel was there for me. After what seemed like an eternity, I reached my hand to it. I wasn't able to fully reach it, but then it grabbed my wrist. The same wrist that healed very, very well. It jerked me, and I mean it was a jerk like the jerk you get when you hammer the throttle, pulling a vehicle out with a chain without properly slacking it. Coming back to consciousness was extremely sobering considering my blood alcohol was 0.48. I was tied to a life support machine, and I was freaking out. My heart, at this point, was in and out of rhythm for several hours after awakening. But there was a thought that came from somewhere during that bringing back. *Don't stop breathing.*

I found out later it was one of my family members that said it, but I was not fully back when I received the message. (Thanks for this strength that kept me breathing.) As if this is not weird enough for you, let me make it weirder. My wife was still in high school at the time. We were unmarried. She was 225-ish miles away from me, 120-ish miles from where I went to tech school. She told her ma that day she didn't want to go to school; she had a bad feeling and she didn't know why. Then she got the news and made arrangements to come see me. Written on my wrist, the wrist that I severely burned and the angel grabbed was this: LeAnn. The first name of my wife. It has healed and faded now, but in that moment with my wife who had rushed to see me, I knew I had found my love for life. I think I even asked her to marry me in the hospital (even though I was unable to speak properly for months after this event). I have since healed and thank all involved; you worked a wonder on me. And I also want to say this; thoughts and prayer cards poured in. I will go more through prayers in a later chapter, but I would have never healed as fast as I did without those prayers. No one, and I mean no one, expected the rate at which I healed, and I know it came solely from those prayers. Thank you.

This was a massive turning point in my life from that great suffering, and there was a pit—like the pit I was in—put into my being, and this pit, I could not fill. I still had not found Jesus. It started to consume me slowly but then quickly arose to consume every thought I had. I stopped it for a short period with alcohol, but thankfully, I replaced alcohol quickly with life lessons, which was learning how to farm. (I still am learning.) Alcoholics, I have a message for you. A wise man's father once told him, "If the bottle ever gets a hold of you, check yourself in, cause it's gonna check you out."

The reason we hit the substance is because we cannot fill the void. It is an impossible task, so we are faced with the choice: life or death. (Again, no option C). Substance is a way to avoid life because life is long in suffering (Galatians 5:22–23). Death is the short and easy way out but the true ends of which are not sweet. God is the only thing that can fill the void, and longsuffering will bring your heart true joy (Romans 15:13). It was easy for me to choose life (though I know it' not as easy for everyone) because of how I replaced alcohol. I was learning how to farm. Turns out, God made a farmer for a reason. Just ask Paul Harvey why God made a farmer; he knows what I'm talking about.

There was a lot about these learnings which came from every source imaginable that brought my thoughts closer to God but not unto God. Then, when I tapped out those sources, the feeling came back and consumed me once more. And the feeling was this: why did God, out of all the peoples in the world, choose to save me? It ate away at me night and day. I finally broke down one day and looked up at God and said, "Answer me, tell me why. I cannot stand living like this anymore." And these are the events that followed.

Before I called out to God, I was reading Genesis and Revelation—the beginning and the end. And after calling out to God one day, I had a thought. I wonder what other people think of these books. I would like to hear what they had to say. So I went to YouTube and typed in Genesis. The very first video was Kent Hovind's creation seminar series. I said to myself, "self who's this joker?" I swiped past him to a video called Genesis theory or something like that. (White rabbit?) It was eight hours long. It contained a bunch of creation theories. The very first speaker got the majority of the time. He was a tall, blonde-haired, blue-eyed, well-spoken fellow. And I sat there and listened in awe. Never listened to the rest of the video—just him.

After watching that video, I was charged up and my being was crackling with life (Romans 12:1113). It was short lived though. So I watched it again and again, and the feeling lasted shorter and shorter. Finally, I said to self, "I got to know who this guy is."

I missed it every time I watched that video, because within the first ten seconds of him coming on that video, he says, "Hi, my name is Kent Hovind. I believe the Bible is literally true and scientifically accurate."

I said to myself again (let's face it, some of the best conversations we have are with self, and if we ever get into an argument, we always win), "Kent Hovind…Kent Hovind…why is that name so familiar?" Then I looked up at God and said, "Really, God? Kent Hovind? The guy whose videos I have been passing up all this time." Yup, God had sent me a comforter, and I wasn't listening (John 14:16). That is a huge part of knowledge—the willingness to listen. I recommend that series. It is a very well put together thought. I'm not saying it's his way or the highway, but he was the man that took off my blindfold and brought God back into the light for me to see. He also set me on this final path which lead to Jesus.

Now, this final path is controversial to Christians. I want you to know and know this: God has a specific path for each and every one of us to get us to Jesus. This is because each one of us are unique and require a very specific order to untangle the mess we have gotten ourselves into. So for me, the order was Genesis, Exodus, Revelation, Kent Hovind (Sorry, I had to put him in here), Numbers, Leviticus, Deuteronomy, Judges, 1 Kings, 2 Kings, Psalms, Job, Books of Enoch, Lost books of Adam and Eve, Jasher, Jubilees, and finally, the nail in the coffin was the gospel of John (2 Peter 3:9).

The two that were the most important to me were the books of Enoch and John. The cause and the effect laid before my very eyes. It was then I knew I was surrounded and consumed by sin and needed a way out. It was what Jesus did for the thief on the cross that did me in. In the last moments of that thief's and Jesus's life, Jesus saved one more for heaven's sake. This last act of compassion did it for me. He treated His neighbor in pain and suffering as Himself. This didn't come at any small expense. I then knew Jesus was a real part of Christianity (to me at least), and I was now riddled with thoughts whether to believe or not to believe; that was the question. And my surrender was to this line of thought. I cannot disprove anything Jesus said or did; therefor, my path to heaven is right through Jesus as He said. Now, I am terrified that Jesus (and not self) holds my key to Heaven, and that is the fear of the LORD! And this fear of the Lord will give you great knowledge and, to the holy, understanding. After all, what is knowledge without the understanding of it? So I will finish this chapter by saying, "Search the scripture on this one." It's a theme that is just under the radar. All who wrote the scriptures feared the LORD GOD and obtained great understanding for Heaven's sake!!!

CHAPTER 6

KEY OF LOVE

Now that I have hopefully broken into your heart a little with my story, please allow me to break in it again. I said in the last chapter the fear of the Lord is the beginning of knowledge, but let me show you what the understanding is.

Let us start at the beginning. "For this is the message that ye heard from the beginning, that we should love one another" (1 John 3:11). When God created us, he gave us many blessings (Genesis 1:27–31). That really, to me, sounded like a whole lot of love, but when Adam and Eve sinned by eating from the tree of the knowledge of good and evil, then came fear, and this is why (Genesis 3:16–19). God has all the power and punished them according to what they had done. That is a terrifying thing, to have to stand before All-Powerful God, give your testimony, and receive your due reward. There is something, though, that can take this fear away. It is truth and strength for all.

> Whosoever shall confess that Jesus is the Son of God, God dwelleth in him, and he in God. And we have known and believed the love that God hath to us. God is love; and he that dwelleth in love dwelleth in God, and God in him. Herein is our love made perfect, that we may have boldness in the day of judgment: because as he is, so

31

are we in this world. There is no fear in love; but perfect love casteth out fear: because fear hath torment. He that fearth is not made perfect in love. We love him, because he first loved us. (1John 4:15–19)

So this story I am about to tell you occurred after I put to rest my conflict with coming to fully believe in Jesus. The first spring my wife and I moved north to the iron band, we had a nicely colored bull calf. It was not overwhelmingly large for a bull calf, but its color was very appealing. It had black fur with orange tips on its hair. It also had orange in the ears, like British whites have black in the ears (fall orange, not hunting orange). I wanted to keep it to try to get that color back into my herd. *Felix* never seems to happen to a farmer, and these are the events that followed.

In the late fall of that year, when the frost was setting in, I went out to check my herd. Out of the corner of my eye, I saw what looked like a black spot in the manure that was building up. As I got closer, I realized that it was my calf laying there, barely alive and barely with his head above the semi-thawed manure. I grabbed him in my arms and carried him into the barn, manure covered and all. I built for him a bed of hay and dried him as quickly as I could. When I got him dry, I picked up his head and looked into his eyes. A moment hit me. The moment told me this, as if God Himself were speaking it to me through that calves' eyes, "There is nothing you can do. This is what I do." The world becomes much different when you are responsible for a life; the value of life greatly changes.

So I, overtaken by that thought, proceeded to run through the motions. Get the penicillin, warm water, calf replacer, grain, and get him warm. There was no response to any of it. That calf was dead, and he just didn't know it yet. I didn't know what to do, so I did the only thing that made sense to me and that was comfort him as best I could. I then picked him up in my arms. I looked up at God and said, "He's ready to go, and I can't do it. Please help."

Shortly thereafter, he died in my arms. It was love, the lesson God was teaching me, and I have no control over death. So to defeat death, the key is love. If God truly did not love us, He would have left us to death. I think God's greatest power, even though He can do anything, is to forgive us of our sins. That is a hard thing to do: forgive someone of wrongdoing against you. Out of love comes forgiveness, and out of forgiveness comes love. Now, I don't want you to think I'm saying make love not war like some have protested. There is a time to make war, a time for peace, a time to love and a time to hate; all have their seasons (Ecclesiastes 3:1–9). What I am saying though is if you want to love, you truly have to understand that all is vanity. Everything you do under the sun is vanity and vexation of spirit (Ecclesiastes 1:14). This means that which is for yourself is for nothing. When it hits you like it hit me, the weight of the world will fall to the ground.

I'll give you an example. I have helped build eleven houses now, and I don't get to live in anyone of them, yet I have retained the knowledge to build up my own house. Yet, when I die, it will pass on to the next generation, and all plans I have will cease (Ecclesiastes 2:18–20). This was when I first obtained the concept that all is vanity. It only took a decade for me to understand what this means. I was old enough to say, "No, I don't want to help," but I helped anyway. This was most likely loving my neighbor to lend a helping hand. This helping has continued with me my whole life, but this building of eleven houses set it firm in my foundation. Within the eleven houses, there were various tasks to complete, and from this, I am now called the "Zack of all trades" by my family. This knowledge has helped me build up my farm. You see how loving your neighbor can really give you a leg up in the world. These things are only a few—and I mean a few—things that come from love.

I will leave you with this last thought. We start life with absolutely nothing, God gives us His love and everything we need. When those moments come, will you accept His love and gifts to you and build up by returning that love to Him? My favorite book is Ecclesiastes. It took me completely by surprise, and it found me by an accident (after listening to Solomon's song on YouTube, it popped on, and I couldn't shut it off after hearing the first chapter). Yet, when I heard that book, so much of my life started to make even more sense. (Please read it if you get a chance.) I am starting to believe my life has been written by Gods word (spoiler).

And to my father, I write, you must stop worrying about the things you have no control over. Our fathers have left the place of their origin to seek another. This is because every man must cleave to his wife, acquire a place, eat from his own fig tree, drink from his own cistern, and become the prince of his own land. This is the will of the LORD God, and blessed are we to receive it. And it is by His will all things are done. Stop putting you faith in me and start putting it in Him. The life of the flesh is momentary, but the life of the spirit will be eternal, and if you don't receive the gift of Jesus, we will part after this momentary life of the flesh and never see each other again. All things that are of man will perish, but the earth will abideth forever. If God needs a farmer, He will send a farmer. If He needs a builder, He will send a builder. A wise man leaves an inheritance to his children's children, but it is God that will send for that child. A wise son maketh a glad father, because one day, the son will lift his father back up. Go back to the beginning, because this life of the flesh will not last. The woods I will see you in is not of this earth; it is in the wilderness of Heaven. For a man once said to me, "God made it that way for a reason."

I then say to him, "God has done all for you for His reasons. He absolutely loves you no less than any other. There may be a little Job in your story, but even Job received the reward of heaven for his patience."

And from my love who gave this to me, I write now the "Key of Love." Love is not someone you can stand to be with, it's someone you can't stand to be without (Rafael Ortiz).

And I write, "Love is great. God is love.

CHAPTER 7

— ❦ —

KEY OF WORDS

> In the beginning was the Word, and the Word
> was with God, and the Word was God.
>
> —John 1:1

T his book may be a little overbearing at times. So I decided to have a little fun for you. I'm gonna show you some fun ways to pass the time. I'll use names and get to the message later in this chapter. First name basis only. My son's name is Liam, and his four fathers from his dad's side are Zachary, David, Walter, and Stanley. And now, I will define their literal meanings.

- Stanley—dweller near a stony clearing
- Walter—army ruler
- David—beloved
- Zachary—God has remembered
- Liam—helmet of will

Now, let me explain how this works. My son Liam is a helmet of will, and that is no joke. This kid has absolutely no fear whatsoever. He's three and he's worse than an energizer bunny on overdrive. Myself, I got into some spiritual trouble, as in the spirit had left the body shortly. But God remembered me and sent me an angel to bring me back. Thanks, God, by the way.

My father, David, has done many good works and made good money for the county. He served as forester. In so doing, he was beloved by many as being a good man.

Grandpa Walter was a battle axe, from what my dad has described him as. He would always tell him what to do.

Stanley was the first of my father's father to make it to the United States of America. The Polish settlers of that community landed in solid bedrock. So guess what kind of clearing he lived in? This is describing each one of them. Now, watch this.

I, whom God has remembered, am extremely willed. So much so that I, through the Spirit of God, wrote this book. I, through actions of righteousness, am beloved. I, like my father, represent interests of people, and through those actions, they like me. I really like war strategy games, movies, and books. I am definitely fascinated and fixated on warfare (especially medieval warfare). My only dislike is lives lost in conflict. God has definitely geared me for leadership of something. Guess, just guess, where I live as a farmer. I moved twenty-seven miles north, and I'm still in a stony clearing. Now, watch this.

- Lois—more desirable
- Margaret—pearl
- LeAnn—light; beautiful women
- Zhanna—God is gracious

Sorry it's not as complete a list. And I don't know the exact details on this one, but consider this: A more desirable pearl, which is a light beautiful woman, by the grace of God was given to a man who God has remembered. Do you get the significance of God's word yet? This is considering all the things that had to come to be in order for God's Word to be fulfilled (and my wife was adopted. These are her birth mother's name and daughters' names). Now, for the sake of time, I'm not going to include our whole lineage. I will do one more and then the message. These are the Bible's good line of men.

- Adam—The first Man
- Seth—is appointed

- Enosh—a mortal man of
- Kenan—sorrow.
- Mahalalel—The glory of God
- Jared—shall descend
- Enoch—dedicated
- Methuselah—his death shall bring
- Lamech—those brought low
- Noah—comfort and rest.

And how bout now? Are you starting to see the message? You cannot run nor hide from fulfillment of God's word (Joshua 21:45). He is the infinite *jäger* of mankind. And let this thought conflict you; we will fulfil God's Word to the letter. Many Christians will say, "We are incapable of fulfilling the law."

But I say to you, "That is fulfillment of the scriptures" (1 Timothy 1:7–11). Which is to say, when God said we, by our own accord, cannot fulfil the law (Romans 3:23), His word was fulfilled. When He said one would come to stomp on Satan's head (Genesis 3:15), His word was fulfilled. When God sent His Son to allow the world remission of sin (Matthew 26:28), His word was fulfilled, and when God said He's coming down to wage war against the sinners (Revelation 19:11–21), His word is still fulfilled.

Now, you might be saying to yourself that hasn't happened yet, its waiting to be fulfilled, and to that I say, "Do you or do you not believe in the Word of God?" Because if you do, you cannot say that, because saying that is disbelieving because of the doubt you're spreading. This will lead you to become (2 Peter 3:4). When you believe in God, His Word is fulfilled, whether it be done or waiting to be done. Stop waiting for His coming and start preparing, because when He comes, many will say, "It's about time, God."

And I will say, "Never doubted You for a second. Your people and I are ready to go when You're ready to take us home."

Doubt is the atheists' greatest weapon, which has lead them to this belief. "We don't believe in God." I'm sorry, but who did you say you don't believe in, and how did you come to know of Him? The real reason that people stop believing in God, however, is that believing in God would set the standard to God's standard of life. Then there would be no lust for self-interests, and believers in no God can't stand the thought of God telling them what to do. So they believe that believing in no God will somehow make Him unreal. I say to that you can try, try, and try some more, and let me know how that went for you when you find yourself standing before the Lord. Try explaining to Him. Try imagining explaining to Him that "You're not real, I have not believed in You, therefore, You are not real" (Revelation 20:11). Ask Judas if the holes in Jesus's hands were real enough for him! (John 20:27).

Oh my lord, I have gotten off track fast here, so let's get back to God's Word as it pertains to you and I. I said in the last chapter that I am starting to believe that my life is already written by God's Word, and I believe I will fulfil it to the letter, but the free will aspect needs to be addressed (Galatians 5:13). I believe free will is the choice to do God's word or rebel against God's word (1 Corinthians 10:13). Here's where it gets tricky. When we Christians do God's will, part of me feels as though there is no space for free will in what we do; however, when I look at my house and compare it to other Christian's houses, yeah, there's the free will. They are not the same. I have come to believe that we Christians are in one accord of Christ Jesus, and our free will is the uniqueness of how we complete that will that God has assigned us. This could include anything, and here comes the wondrous argument. Faith, works, and works of faith. I will be referencing Paul's writings versus James's writings here. I really like Paul's writings; however, I prefer James's (a little bit easier to understand). These two men may have been talking to two different types of people, but the goal was the same (bring them to Jesus). We're gonna have to start with some definitions and then some understandings of those definitions.

- Faith—your conviction (Hebrews 11:1).
- Works—a task you do to benefit yourself.
- Work of Faith—a task you do to benefit the Lord God's Will/Word, which should be your faith.

Faith is what I believe, and I believe that Jesus Christ died for my sin to be forgiven, and God is the Creator, and God and Jesus are one (John 10:30; 1 Peter 3:18; John 10:14–15).

Work is tasks for an employer. I perform forty hours a week to earn a wage that I might buy whatever my heart desires for my own pleasure (Ecclesiastes 2).

Work of faith. Boy, isn't it a work of faith that I believe in Jesus's sacrifice, and even God without having been able to actually prove their existence or see that sacrifice in person? (Hebrews 11:1)

There are many works of faith, and they come only when the spirit leads. When the spirit is leading, you will accomplish a work of faith. Let's face truth here; the spirit will lead us cows to water, but the flesh is required to do the work and drink. I hear Christians say, "All you need is faith in Jesus."

I have no idea how this thought explains James when he says, "Even so, faith, if it hath not works, is dead, being alone." Nor do I see how it pertains to Paul when he said, "No man is justified by works of the law." These men are saying the same thing.

I will start with James. Review James chapter 2. All of it, several times. Again, he said, "Even so faith, if it hath not works is dead, being alone" (James 2:17). He believed this so much he expanded it by saying, "Yea, a man may say, Thou hast faith, and I have works: shew me thy faith without thy works, and I will shew thee my faith by my works" (James 2:18). Now, James here is not talking about works of the law nor works in general; he's referring to works of faith which, through the spirit, he is performing out of love and the love of God.

Paul is specifically referencing the works of the law, and he was correct in saying that no man aside from Jesus can be fulfilled by those works (fulfillment of scriptures) (Galatians 2:16; Matthew 5:17). Here is where it gets interesting. Paul loves referencing circumcision. So I'm gonna try to make a clean circumcision joke here. No man goes to his brother and says, "Hey, man lets chop the tips of our members off."

And no brother turns to his brother and says, "Hey, man, that sounds like a great idea! Let's do it." This is nuts. We would have never done this on our own, knowing of pain, but when God makes a covenant with man and tells man to do this work/deed out of obedience/love for God to acquire a great thing from God, then man has to do this, and when man loves and is obedient to God, he is willing to do this thing for God to show God that, "Hey I am obedient/loving of you, God, even though this thing is gonna cause me or my eight-day-old much pain and suffering."

Paul uses this and says, "It is not the circumcision of the member but rather the circumcision of the heart that God had accepted and sent Jesus to help with that circumcision" (Romans 2:24–29). This work of faith was performed to the flesh by the spirit out of love, and for the love, of God.

I will give one more example, and then I will pull Paul and James together. Cain cheated God by giving Him a crap offering of what was not his best yield (Genesis 4:3, 5–7). Cain's name literally means "hater." He gave a poor offering out of hate. He killed his brother out of hate (Genesis 4:8). Abel means literally "breathing spirit" and didn't when he was slain by his brother. His spirit took a good deep celestial breath, and his blood cried out to the Lord God! (Genesis 4:10). Abel's offering and acceptance by God (Genesis4:4) made Cain jealous, and Abel was righteous insomuch that the offering came from his loving heart, because he loved God with all his heart, might, and soul so much so that he gave the best of his yield. That is a work of faith. To confirm this all, read Hebrews chapter 11 and Genesis chapter 4.

This is where I will tie it all together here. Love is the work of faith, and so is obedience. (Willingness is love, and obedience versus tolerance is to tolerate.) It is my conviction that these two words are one in the same. How are you obedient without love, and how do you love without obedience? I cannot explain, without God's understanding of love, what love is or why we do it, and I cannot explain why we are obedient without God's understanding of obedience, what it is to be obedient, or why we do it. All I do know is that the spirit takes me to these words and holds me in accordance to God's literal meaning of these words, and I believe it is because they are the will of God for us to do. I think Paul and James were both stating that the work of faith was love God in all that you do, and with your faith in Jesus, the hard-hearted (tolerant) shall be remade soft-hearted (willing) so the true love of thine neighbor can take place, and how can this not be a work of love/obedience? (Ezekiel 11:14–21).

> Hearken, my beloved brethren, Hath not God chosen the poor of this world rich in faith, and heirs of the kingdom which he hath promised to them that love him? But ye have despised the poor. Do not rich men oppress you, and draw you before the judgment seats? Do not they blaspheme that worthy name by which ye are called? If ye fulfil the royal law according to the scripture, thou shalt love thy neighbor as thyself, ye do well. (James 2:5–8)

> (Paul) Render therefore to all their dues: tribute to whom tribute is due; custom to whom custom; fear to whom fear; honour to whom honour. Owe no man any thing, but to love one another: for he that loveth another hath fulfilled the law. (Romans 13:7–8, parentheses mine)

If you are still having trouble with works of faith, check out these references: Matthew 5:17–20, Matthew 7:11–29, and Isaiah 42:21.

*Now note I wrote this part here after I wrote this whole chapter, and I'm almost done with this book, but I just came up with an answer to the question I stated at the beginning of this small section. I stated I have no idea what it means when people say all you need is faith in Jesus. It's actually saved by grace alone which comes from Ephesians 2:8–9. Ephesians 2:8–10 Paul has separated the three: faith, works, and works of faith, the greatest of which are love God and love your neighbor as thyself (1 John 4:20). He's saying through moving, calling, and acknowledging Jesus Christ (grace), you are saved by your belief in Him (faith), and then you will be able to do the works of faith (love) that stem from a softening (willingness) of the heart. Know that this is extremely hard for me to say, so I will try my best. Your works will be a reflection of your faith. If your faith is not there, your works will reflect that, and if your faith is there, your works will also reflect that. If you still think that faith or grace through faith will save you alone, then I ask you after your belief in Jesus lifts our guilt you and I obtained after transgressing the commandments of God, what then will He judge us by? Does he judge faith or works or both? And how? (James 2:14). This war of faith versus works is a major err. Jesus came to take away our sins through His sacrifice *and make the hard heart soft!* What good then is making the hard heart soft if it only takes believing in Jesus to be able to get to heaven? I'm going to go on a mass killing spree, but you know what, it's all gonna be OK for me because I proclaim to believe in Jesus while I'm killing people! (I'm not going to kill people, so don't worry if you think I will, or have I already?) (Matthew 5:22). Do you really think a person could actively do this and Jesus would forgive him while still doing it? Because this is exactly where this thought leads. I'm not under the law of sin and death, because I am saved by grace alone. Another way to say that is I can do whatever I want because I got Jesus. What good is faith if it couldn't produce good works? That faith is dead, for it is in good works our faith shines, and through Jesus Christ, our bad works are forgiven and our way of sinning is rebuked (Luke 8:4–15). Paul references the circumcision of one's heart more than any other person in the Bible. That's because it's that important. That is a work of faith; to acknowledge that we are full of sin and call to Jesus for forgiveness is a work because it is required that you do it. I really like Paul's writings, but sometimes, you have to make sure what you think he is saying holds up to the rest of scripture. (2 Peter 3:14–18). "For as the body without the spirit is dead, so faith without works is dead also" (James 2:26). Don't have blind faith, brothers and sisters, because if we do, we will have nothing to show our faith by, and Jesus will say, "Depart ye that work iniquity."

How would you explain the faith of all those in Hebrews chapter 11? By their works? How would you explain your faith? By your works?

This war of faith versus works is a major err because the whole point is to get the good works of all people flowing again. If you, on your own, and I, on my own, could love God and our neighbors, there would truly be no guilt to have to lift. That's why, now, it takes Jesus and faith to love your neighbor as yourself.

Faith is proven by works and it is only possible with a soft heart.

If faith is the substance of things hoped for, the evidence of things not seen, then how did the elder receive good report? It is impossible to separate faith, works, and heart because faith will make the hard heart soft, and from a soft heart shall good works be produced.

I'm going to one up everyone who says grace alone, and even Paul, even though I think this is really what Paul meant, by saying I am saved by a soft heart which I got when I took a leap of faith, calling Jesus Christ of Nazareth for the forgiveness of my sins so that I could work love to my neighbors and my God!

I think I found my definition of love. Love—the work reflected from one's faith that comes from the heart.

I'm going to end this by saying again that the softening of your heart, faith, and works are the same because of how they are tied together, and stating each one of these can save you is correct, but they never are truly alone.

If you want to give credit where credit is due, be saved by Jesus Christ alone!

Wow, that was a weight off my chest, but again, let's get this derailed train back on track with God's Word.

In the beginning, God made a place to put things, and He made the things to put in the place. Then He must have thought to Himself, *Self, it's dark in here*, so He said, "Let there be light," and then He could see everything, and after separating the light from the dark, He said, "This is good."

Folks, watch this.

God created, by His word, a place to put things for the things He put in place, then He created, by His Word, a light to see things, then He separated the night and day to make a complete day one. Then He formed a firmament by His Word by which the waters could be separated, then, after He created heaven, it was the completion of the second day. Then God gathered the waters by His Word so dry land could appear, and the dry Earth, by God's Word, brought forth all the plants by the seeds of their kinds, and this was the completion of day three. Then God, by His Word, put lights in the firmament of Heaven to make day and night, signs and seasons, days, years, give light unto the Earth, the sun, the moon, the stars, and He even gave the light rule over day and night to make the completion of day four. Then God, by His word, brought forth the sea creatures in the gathered waters and the birds in the firmament, and blessing them by His word, they brought forth abundantly. This was the completion of day five. Then God, by His word, created the beast, the cattle, the creeping things, the man, and then the woman, and God blessed them by His word, allowing them to multiply, and He also gave dominion to man over His living creature kingdom, and man and woman were to eat only the herbs, the fruits, and the animals and birds were to eat only the green herbs. God saw everything was *very good!* The completion of the sixth day. Then God, by His word, blessed the seventh day as the day of rest, having completed His work, and He rested. The completion of the seventh day.

Now, again, I'm paraphrasing here. I could make this argument. God, by His word, created space, matter, light, day, night, heaven, outer space (or inner space, depending from where your standing), and with that, the atmospheres, the dry earth, seas, grass and seeds of their kind, herbs and seeds of their kind, fruit trees and seeds of their kind, stars, the sun, the moon, sea life with reproduction after their kind, birds with reproduction after their kind, living land creatures with reproduction after their kind (beasts, cattle, creeping things), man and then women with reproduction of our kind, order of dominion, order of things to eat for all, rest from labor. That this is how it was, but I'm not smart enough to approve this shorter list as I wrote it; it could be wrong (I'm just being honest), but I'm gonna put the train in the station. If the order of things made were not in the order God spoke them to be made, it would not be absolute truth. The key of words is that God's Word is absolute. By God's hard work, we have order to things, and all things are in their order, but when man, by his works, departs from God's Word, disorder emerges, and sin, unlawfulness, evil, and transgression will destroy God's very good estate that the earth was in. I know you may or may not believe in what the books of Enoch said, and I will address this book in a later chapter, but even he said that, in the time of the sinners, everything comes out of its place (Enoch chapter 80, 81, and 82). Return, therefore, to the Word God spoke, and you shall again return to the *very good estate!*

> Remember therefore from whence thou are fallen, and repent, and do the first works; or else I will come unto thee quickly, and will remove thy candlestick out of his place, except thou repent. (Revelation 2:5)

CHAPTER 8

— ⚜ —

KEY OF EVIL

M an, that last chapter was a chapter and a half to write, and this one might be too (still contemplating what to write for this key). Sorry, I'm having one of those Matthew 10:18–20 moments. OK, here goes.

Caution! I will have you start by looking up lyrics to the song "Washington is Next" authored by Megadeth. Caution. There is one bad word at the end of this song. You've been warned! (You can listen to the song also, if you'd like. You don't have to do either if you don't want to.)(Ephesians 4:29)

OK, now that we're in the mood, I would like to say this is not going to be a key saying this is evil, that is evil, that is evil, this is evil, and that's definitely evil. This going to be about structure (Romans 16:19). Because the key of evil is about how it comes and goes.

Let's do an exercise. You'll need a sheet of papyrus. Paper will work also. Get a pen too so that I may show you the pen is mightier than the sword. Put a one at the top middle of the paper, then two twos below the one, with the one in the middle. Then three threes below the twos, with the twos in between the threes. Go all the way to ten tens following this pattern. It should be shaped like a pyramid. Then draw lines around the edges of the numbers in the shape of a pyramid. Then draw another pyramid ninety degrees to the right, and draw a circle around it. It's satanic, I tells you.

I'm messing with you a little. Turn the page over, and let's start again. Do the first step one through ten in the shape of a pyramid. This time, draw lines only from the ones to the tens and stop (no bottom line through the tens). This is the structure of evil, and I will show you how it comes and goes in this chapter (1 John 5:18–19).

Now, I want you to notice there is one one. This is the devil. He is at the top. He deceives everyone and draws them into his temple (Isaiah 14). When he draws them in, then there are two twos only. Instead of the twos being Adam and Eve, they are his closest living subordinates. And if a two shall die, then a three will take his or her place and so on and so forth.

Now, let's build up this wicked empire. Continue the numbers up to fifteen fifteens and continue the line from the tens to the fifteens. Notice that the ones, twos, threes, fours, fives, sixes, sevens up to the fourteens have no way out. They are locked in by the walls on left and right, and they are also blocked in by the numbers above and below. The only way out is death, in which case, the lower will shift up.

Now, notice the bottom. It is open on the bottom. Those who are working for heaven's sake, this is your way in. This is the weakest portion. This is also why evil keeps evolving. The more it evolves, the more it captures. A man today who is righteous may tomorrow see the latest and greatest thing and want it, falling from grace.

Finally, let's rip this empire down. Take out any of the two fifteens right next to each other, and what do you notice? You should see a way to pull out a fourteen because he has no fifteen to his left or right; however, if you pull that fourteen out, you cannot pull out a thirteen because he is still locked by the other fourteen. Triangles are very strong structures. The devil's plan is also contrary to God's Word. God's Word is exponential and will deliver your mind to freedom, whereas the devil's is, one at a time, imprisoning your mind so you become his slave. The devil is trying to build a wedge big enough to wedge God out of place so he can take His place. It's not going to work though, so back to bringing down the evil empire. Take out all of the fifteens and take the line back to the fourteens. Then so on and so forth back to one.

Now, that you have taken his army away one tier at a time, put a bottom on him. Lock him in a pit and throw away the key so he can't deceive the nations anymore (Revelation 20:3). This is how evil comes and goes. We Christians must keep trying to clear the temple of that old serpent. Many Christians want to attack the devil on top, but he is so protected that no one in any lifetime except God will ever reach him, and how many of God's people went up against Goliath and just one smote him on the head. (1 Samuel 17).

Jesus knew this, and even though He was the last man to bruise Satan's head, Jesus went out for the people (Luke 5:4). He went for the bottom and pulled many upon many and is still, to this day, pulling many out. That is our battleground. Now that I have shown you this, I want to pull a few more thoughts in here. I am gonna give to you the deception of the devil, and knowing this is of the greatest importance (Matthew 4:7–11).

The devil said to Jesus, who he had taken to a high exceeding mountain, "All these things will I give to you if you fall down and worship me."

Then Jesus said, "Get thee hence, Satan, for it is written, thou shalt worship the Lord thy God, and Him only shall thou serve." The deception is that Satan gets you to believe that he owns everything, and if you worship him, he'll give you anything you want. If he comes around, tell him to get lost, or better yet, ask him if he has accepted Jesus Christ as his Lord and Savior. That usually burns them out. There is a right way and a wrong way to go about living, and it's probably going to cost you money. *Pay your dues!* (Ecclesiastes 5:4–6) Owe no man anything, and the devil will have no hold over you. God protects the righteous in one way or another, and even though trouble comes your way He will provide a way and He will lead you by the hand if you let Him.(Corinthians 10:13, 2 Corinthians 4:8–9, 1 Thessalonians 5:23–24, 2 Thessalonians 3:3, Deuteronomy 31:6, Isaiah 41:10, Psalms 5:11, 20:1, 23:1–6, 34:19, 46:1, 138:7, 140:4, 2 Samuel 22:3–4, John 10:28–30) God owns His creation; give Him His due. God because He hath created this place also hath the power to judge it and give unto each according to his work whether be good or bad. (2Cothintians 5:10) Evil is very simple, follow the money flow. If you get stuck doing this ask this very simple question "and who gave them their money?" This question will take you straight to the top. (Ezekiel chapter 28) I can hardly image a world without money but I know one can exist, and under God it would be perfect.

Now, I would like to speculate on how evil goes from none to its final phase. It is my conviction that the four horseman are actually the plot/stages of evil. This may be a hard thing to explain, but I'm gonna give it my best shot. Read Matthew 24:3, and then read all chapter twenty-four.

Matthew 24:4–5: The white horseman with a bow. This, to me, represents the lies that come to destroy the faith God's people have for Him because a crook (bow) will make that which is straight crooked, and that which is made crooked can knot be made straight (Ecclesiastes 1:15). This is the most powerful of the horsemen, because this will shake the foundation of human living. This horseman is tied to every aspect of life and will corrupt every aspect of human civilization (not so civil after all). They who ride with the white horseman will use lies to their advantage and claim they only want to be equal, but what they really seek is your conformance (Romans 12:1–2). This is a sickness above all else, and it has brought every empire to ashes. As I said before, my country has the lie tax supported. Evolution is the lie that absolutely destroys absolute. This theory has been just that for almost 6000-ish years (Genesis 3–5. Ye shall be as Gods). (The approximate historical length of the creation by the Bible.) You would have thought by now it would be proven law, but people have faith that evolution is truth, so they have justification in their minds of their actions with no standing consequence (that is to say, standing before God and confessing their transgressions). (They better be absolutely right.) The lie is that we can become equal to God or higher than (Colossian 2:8; Mark 9:35–42; Isaiah 8:8–22; 2 Timothy 4:3–4).

Matthews 24:6: The red horseman with a great sword. This, to me, represents wars and rumors of wars. When you tell people we are the gods of our own creation, bad things happen. We establish a value to each people's life, and those closest to the real God are the first to be exterminated. When someone else has what we want, we take it by force, and the most evolved races determine how all live under them. Opposition must be vanquished. If we cannot control them, kill them 'til there is control. As many as it takes. There must be order!

War sucks. Ask any of our American service members that served in the Middle East or are currently serving there. I don't think they would have much good to say about those conditions. War is a hardship you carry for life. (Service members having a hard time, please hang in there. You have a God above that loves you more than anything you can image, and I thank you with all my heart for your service to our country.) With the lie, the world will become engulfed in war, and it's mostly to eliminate anything that poses a threat to the perfect human (devil) imagined world (Revelation 13:10).

Matthew 24:7–9: The black horseman with scales. This to me represents the world coming out of balance. There are many jobs to be done, and if you're not free to do them all, there are not enough provisions to go around, and if there are not enough people to do the jobs, there are really not enough provisions to go around. The free market of the USA ensured that each individual has enough, and if they have more, they can share and sell it freely, and if they don't produce enough, they can buy what they need. Not so when this horseman comes, because you will be expected to give your life to feed another (Ecclesiastes 2:26). When humans and the devil rule you absolutely, there is never enough to go around. There will be very bad things that come with this unbalance. Famines in which many will starve and die will come, and pestilence with it. Famine and pestilence are one in the same because your body needs nutrition to avoid sickness, and sickness needs nutrition to heal you from sickness. None truer is this statement: don't let the salesman tell you different (Mark 5:24–34; Matthew 4:1–4).

Matthew 24:10: The pale horseman death. This is the evil continuous I spoke of, and if we get to this horseman again, who brings the greatest of suffering, we are done. I believe this was the state of the earth right before the flood (Genesis 6). There's not too much to say about this; there will be nothing good, just death continuous (Isaiah 65).

I have changed my mind about the length of this chapter and will end it as the beginning of the next chapter after this last reference. I don't want to give evil anymore of your time!

This reference is from *Kung Fu Panda 2*, produced by DreamWorks.

> Shen: You were wrong, soothsayer! We sail to victory tonight. Your magic panda is clearly a fool!
>
> Soothsayer: Are you certain it is the panda that is the fool? You just destroyed your ancestral home, Shen!
>
> Shen: A trivial sacrifice...when all of China will be my reward.
>
> Soothsayer: Then will you finally be satisfied? Will the subjugation of the whole world make you feel better?
>
> Shen: It's a start. I was also thinking of converting the basement into a dungeon.
>
> Soothsayer: The cup you choose to fill has no bottom. It's time to stop the madness.
>
> Shen: And why on earth would I do that?
>
> Soothsayer: So your parents can rest in peace.
>
> Shen: My parents... hated me. Do you understand? They—they wronged me. And... I will make it right.
>
> Soothsayer: They loved you. They loved you so much that having to send you away killed them.
>
> Shen: The dead exist in the past. And I must attend to the future. Set the soothsayer free. She is no use to me.
>
> Soothsayer: Goodbye, Shen. I wish you happiness.
>
> Shen: Happiness must be taken. And I will take mine.

Evil is easy to understand because it is so well written about. God really wanted all of us to understand why we do it and how it progressively gets worse. To the progressives, I ask, what does the perfect world look like? And then I say, "That doesn't sound good to me." If the word holds its meaning, then what are we progressing toward, God's? Like I said, the minds of darkness are easy because it is so well documented in the Bible. A good place to start is Romans 1–3.

Righteousness exalteth a nation: but sin is a reproach to any people. (Proverb 14:34)

CHAPTER 9

— ❧ —

KEY OF GOOD

So the end of the last and the beginning of this chapter will be a verse, and it goes, "If my people who are called by my name, shall humble themselves, and pray, and seek my face, and turn from their wicked ways; then will I hear from heaven, and will forgive their sin, and heal their land (2 Chronicles 7:14). Christ-tians (a people whom have received Christ), Israel (may God prevail), and all other folks who perceive this world to be evil know this promise and know it well; that no matter how dark the days get, God's promise He made us here will never cease. You need only say, "God, I was wrong. Forgive me." Believe this or not, this is a very hard thing to do, but affirmation of our sin in and of itself is enough to crack the hardest of hearts, and in so doing, just enough to allow Jesus/God to take hold of you (Ezekiel 36:25–28).

I'll tell you a story. I picked up a very bad sinful habit and carried it for many years. I accepted Jesus fully around the ages of twenty-eight to twenty-nine. When I was twenty-nine, it was the year 2017 AD. This was the year the book Jubilees predicted the end of the world by Enoch's calendar (or Hebrew calendar) which he predicted everyone would stop using. Long story short, there was an end of world prediction on December 2017. (I forget the day.) I was freaking out. Part of me thought it's gonna end quick, and the other part of me thought beginning of the ending. (Yes, it was the year of the great sign in heaven). I even went out and bought some end-of-the-world supplies. (Don't think it would have helped, though.)

So the week before the date, I went cold turkey on my bad habit. I said, "I can't do this anymore. I need to stop." Also, I prayed to Jesus to help me end it. That whole week, I repented from the habit and prayed to Jesus to forgive me. The end date came and went. I'm gonna take a pause here to say again, I affirmed my wickedness and sought the face of Jesus, thinking I was gonna meet Him face to face that date. This was the day my hard heart cracked. I had a couple relapses of this habit, but ultimately, with the power of the Spirit, I ended it all together because that crack grew and grew and grew 'til it couldn't support itself and the stone fell away. I believe the end of the world is going to be the same. Evil is going to grow and grow and grow 'til the Earth can support it no more and the stone will fall away, and it will do so without much human consideration of it.

I know there are many theories as to how we go from this age to the next, if that is what God meant, but it will only take one prayer to Jesus for the world to change, because in that moment of fear for me, I had clarity. Things that were once important to me no longer were because they were going to get me thrown into the lake. I was asking Jesus, who had I never seen, met, and fully believed in, to help me, and He answered and put me on a path to be healed. The earth is the same; when man affirms what he is doing is wrong and asks God for forgiveness, then and only then can the path for healing be set. I do believe there is always a way given from God to be forgiven and healed, but I also believe God will only put up with so much. When evil continuously occurs, I believe God will descend from heaven, and it will be done (away with).

If you are out there, and this is something you're going through, call out to Jesus. Tell yourself this is wrong. Call out and tell yourself everyday 'til you see the path. When you see the path, get on it. Trust in Jesus and Jesus alone to keep you on it, and you will get out. Just have patience.

Please allow me to give you another thought. Jesus/God came into this earth knowing full well what was to happen to Him by His own people, and He fulfilled it. He never ran away from or hid from His destined path He went head first, and when He died on the cross, He did it so that we all could be forgiven of our sins through Him and have the strength of the spirit to help us repent from our iniquities. And this sacrifice is incorruptible in its purity.

If my people, who are called Christians, shall have or show themselves modest or low of one's own importance, request, express, attempt to find Jesus/God personally, and turn from their sinful ways, then will God hear from heaven and will forgive us our sins and heal our land.

I don't know what 2 Chronicles says to you, but this is what it says to me, and I want and need nothing more than to be forgiven, healed, and have an open path to heaven. The "Key of Good" is really this simple; trust Jesus. (Hebrew 11:1–2).

I have one last story regarding this subject. When I was a boy, my mom and stepdad were waging war with one another. It got so bad one day that my stepfather asked me and my brother if we wanted him to leave. The flesh of me knew this man was very rough around the edges, but the flesh had no words to speak. I didn't know Jesus in this young age, but somehow, and in some way, He spoke these words through me, "I don't want you to go." After some ironing out of issues, my stepfather is still a part of this family, and now, he is part of this growing family, and he gets to be a happy grandpa. I am glad that those words came out in that moment because they were righteous, truthful, and exactly the words that needed to be spoken. Trust Jesus!

As I wrote in the last chapter, the good is also easy to understand. You may judge a man by his fruits, but—and here is a big but—you can't condemn them lest you condemn yourself. If you want to know for sure about the characteristics of the good, look at 2 Peter 1.

CHAPTER 10

— ☙ —

KEY OF FAITH

OK, here, I am going to start this chapter with a metaphor. After all, the Bible has to be physically, spiritually, and metaphorically truth, or I wouldn't be so, right?

And the parable I write is this (with hopes it will hold up to scripture).

One day, a man who had knowledge called out to the Lord God from a high mountain, saying, "King of Kings and Lord of Lords, how may I best serve thee?" There was no answer. The man had returned every day for a time, and after much fasting and praying and calling from that high mountain, the Lord God came and spoke.

He said, "Thou may serve Me greatly by moving the high lake on your right to the low valley on your left."

And the man looked to his right and his left and said, "God, this is a big task. How may I do it best?"

God said, "Behind you is a five-gallon pail. I will see you tomorrow," and God left the man to his task. The man looked behind himself, and behold, there was a five-gallon pail. The man flipped the pail and took a seat and looked at the task God had assigned him. The man, overwhelmed by the task, sat and paced and thought many thoughts, and the day had ended and the night began.

The man said to himself, "Self, I will rest and begin tomorrow."

Then when the next day came, God returned and said to the man, "Why hast thou not commenced the task I have assigned thee?"

The man replied, "I was a little overwhelmed by the task, but I will commence on this day."

Then God said, "OK, my son. I will let you at it, and I will see you tomorrow." Again, God had left the man to his task. The man again had looked out and again was so overwhelmed by the task he fell to the ground, cried, and passed out from grief at the portion of the task. He awoke on the third day, and God again had returned. The man didn't say anything to God; he just stood and looked out at the lake and the valley.

God then said to him, "I know thou is overwhelmed, but ye shall now know the understanding of the task. For every day the man doth carry one pail of water from the lake to the valley, his portion shall be complete."

The man humbled, then said, "Is that all it will take to move that lake?"

Then God replied, "No, only your portion of it shall be complete, but in the day that thou convince as many others thy can to take up thy righteous cause, then and only then can the lake be removed, and many shall complete their portion therein."

The man henceforth every morning carried his pail from the lake to the valley and spent the rest of his day convincing others that they should take up the righteous cause to complete their portion thereof. The man became great amongst them, and there was much love for him. They, together, had moved the lake to the valley and had much comfort and rest upon the completion of the great task and built a wonderful city in the remnants of the lake. Even when the rain came and refilled a small portion of the lake, their task to maintain it was small because they righteously labored together. Moral of the story: We may not be able to move hell, but we can certainly move the high water.

Faith is much like this metaphor. The task is a great one and the laborers are very few, and even fewer still will labor therein (Matthew 19:16–26, 7:11–29). Trying to convince someone to leave their comfort zone in today's day and age is next to impossible. There is truly too much convenience. So I will make you aware of a few things and, then I will tell you another story.

In the days of old, the rain didn't come by scientific understanding of weather; it came by prayer to God (James 5:17–18, Zechariah 10:1, Leviticus 26:1–4, Deuteronomy 28:12, Isaiah 30:19–23, 1 Kings 8 33–40, 17, 18:1). Those who believe it now comes from science, consider this; if you believe the rain comes from clouds, who sent the clouds? If you believe the rain comes from the hydrologic cycle, I would say who made the cycle work, and what about the half hydrologic cycle Viktor Schauberger predicted? The answer is the wind which moves the clouds and evaporates the water into the clouds. What drives the winds? The sun's energy drives the winds. What makes the sun's energy and what is energy? (I would ask Nikola Tesla about energy, but his legacy has been erased.) Energy is a dead end field of science by current human standards; we just don't know. The sun's energy is made from nuclear fusion, the combination of hydrogen, and so on and so forth 'til it hits iron, or is it? To that, I have but two questions, the first of science being how do we know the sun isn't a super heavy radioactive element that is shedding both its energy and elements and will then deplete into iron and stabilize much like uranium depletes into lead? The second being who made the sun? Many may say a star nebula, a big combination of gases that somehow compressed in outer space, where there is very little compression at 2.594 degrees Kelvin. Can't be a black hole that compresses it, not even light itself can escape that failed theory, and another question; why is it when you leave the face of the earth toward the sun does it get colder? Shouldn't it get warmer?

I thought we were not too far and just close enough to receive exactly the right amount of heat from the sun, and what about the ellipse the earth rotates on? Winters here aren't too bad at -60 degrees wind chill. Never crossed some folk's minds that this earth we live on was made to do an exact thing (Isaiah 45:16, Psalms 33:6–7, Job 38:4–6) and the sun an exact thing (Genesis 1:16–18), so the temperature could be well maintained. Back to the star nebulas. Who made them? They would have had to come from the big bang, right? Who gave the big bang its energy, and who made everything come from a dot as big as the dot on this page, and who has the power to compress it at that psi? (2 Samuel 22:10; Job 9:8, 26:7,

37:18; Psalms 104:2, 144:5; Isaiah 40:22, 42:5, 45:12, 48:13, 51:13; Jeremiah 10:12, 51:15; Ezekiel 1:22; Zechariah 12:1). And finally, who can make something from nothing? Who has that superpower? (Genesis 1:1.) I believe it was Hitler who coined the big lie propaganda technique.

Here is faith. In the beginning, God, who preceded the beginning, had created space, matter, light, day, night, heaven, outer space (or inner space, depending from where you're standing), and with that, the atmosphere, also the dry earth, seas, grass and seeds of their kind, herbs and seeds of their kind, fruit trees and seeds of their kind, stars, the sun, the moon, sea life with reproduction after their kind, birds with reproduction after their kind, living land creatures with reproduction after their kind (beasts, cattle, creeping things), man and then women with reproduction of our kind, order of dominion, order of things to eat for all, and rest from labor.

I believe in God because if God didn't do it, who the heck is in control of this creation? who hath the power then to control this creation? Who hath the power to maintain it and keep it from falling apart? Who hath the knowledge to create a perfectly functioning creation and assign dominance of all creations? Who knew how to make energy and how to harness it? Who knew how to make heat and how to preserve it? How we are truly held in this earth and can stand upright on its surface. Who knew the density everything must resonate at? Who made the fields coherent? How can light be separated from darkness and affected by magnetism, for that matter? How motion in the aether can generate electricity. Who sends the sun in the day and the moon in the night and determined the appropriate portals and windows by which they should pass through and the phases by which they should shine by? Who had a strong enough voice to carve the hard rocky coasts and a quiet enough whisper to create the human eye? Who hath the true power to fill up my hunger and make me satisfied by fullness of that hunger by His word alone? Who hath the power to renew my mind, heal my sickness, give me my strength, keep me going, cast out my demons, provide me wealth, a wife, a family, a house, good food, clean water, reasonable friends, and life eternal? And finally, who hath the power to answer those prayers and send the needed rain? (You think these questions are good, read God's questions to Job.) Science is not random; the laws are upheld, but they can be broken, and you will not enjoy the results thereof! If you are confused by what I just said, consider this parable: heat and energy are the two sides of the coin, but the coin itself is the key of determination.

So on to my next story. My wife and I were living on our *flowering* farm at the time, and she was bothering me about having kids. After much consideration of the matter, I had concluded two things. How am I going to afford this, and how do I justify raising them in the time we live in? My heart became pretty hard over this matter. I had put faith in God that I was doing the right thing and I had made the right decision, but sometimes, even He puts His unwavering faith on us. This is what He did to me and how it came to be.

A couple of years before me and my wife lived where we now live, my now brother-in-law got a girl pregnant and had a baby girl. It was a pretty big deal to their family. Things happen sometimes, and I remember being there when he announced it. There is a lot of joy now when, then, there was a feeling of disappointment and uncertainly. Just remember, God has a very specific plan for each of us, and it's woven into the grander scheme of things, because when I held my niece, Isis, for the first time, it broke my heart that I didn't want a child of my own to hold. The feeling I had when holding her was overwhelming love. I, then, after this one day of twenty-seven years of days, commenced to baby making and now have two lovely children. And wouldn't you know it, God had provided me with three insurances and made it affordable. Don't even get me started on the year of our great tax return, when I thought I would have to stop farming because I needed a ridiculous amount of return to keep going, and He gave it. My wife and I both cried on that one. Or the first summer in our flowering town when I had twelve acres of pasture and twenty-five beefers to feed that winter, and I prayed and prayed and prayed, and out of nowhere, a man stopped at my house and talked to me for two hours and offered me fifteen of his acres to run and got me another twenty from another lady, and it lead all the way to 125 hayland acres to make hay on. It's kind of a weird joke to me. God won't let me exceed or perish, He holds me in my place (Psalms, all of it). The "Key of Faith" is that faith goes both ways, and God will only ever give you enough to keep you going so that you may never quit, and this connects us all together. He is my rock!

CHAPTER 11

— ☾☽ —

KEY OF PRAYER

All righty then. We are coming to the home stretch. Just a few more chapters to go. I will start this chapter with my personal favorite prayer, and it goes:

God, please let me see the things I need to see that I may speak the things that need be spoken.

Just something I came up with that I'll get to in a later chapter. It means I wish God to show me what He personally would help me to see and that He would be my voice when I need to have one. It has served me pretty well these last four years, and even before I was praying it. Let's start with prayer itself. What is prayer?

Prayer—a solemn request for help or expression of thanks to God or *an object of worship.* (The italicized is something I can do without. I don't worship idols, just the one true God).

So prayer is a formal and dignified request for help or one's thoughts and feelings of thanks to God. So thanks, God, for creating everything we have, that raise I got, the child my wife gave birth to, my wife, and the house to put them in. Or, God, help me to see that which I need to see. To say that which I need to say. I'm in over my head. God, help me.

This prayer thing is definitely not a beauty contest. A lot of people try to outdo the next person. World peace is great, but that's not really all that personal to you. Don't get me wrong, I prayed that God would go with the Cajun Navy and save as many as they could in the last couple of hurricanes which, again, good, but prayer is also a very personal thing. People saving people is a very good thing, world peace…ah…we Christians know the great tribulation is coming, so world peace may not be feasible in this time. The more personal you make it, the more it will come from the soft heart and keep the heart soft.

Pray for neighbors, spouses, children, friends, parents, and any person around you, and you who are needing a little help, because I believe I wouldn't be here if there weren't people surrounding me with their prayers in all my times of need. And above that, pray to God and personally thank Him for those answered prayers and everything He does, especially at the dinner table, for He is the one who truly put the food there. (A good dinner prayer is "Come, Lord Jesus, be our quest, and let these gifts to us be blessed. Amen.")

In my searching of the scriptures, I have found a real good chapter about praying, and it is Matthew chapter 6. I would like to go through this chapter with you. Alms are charity work, and it is saying do not seek glory when you are doing this. It is for those who need it, and God Himself will reward you for doing it (Matthew 6:1–4). When you pray, pray not aloud, seeking self-glory; pray in secret from the heart, and the Father shall hear it (Matthew 6:5–6). When you are praying, do not pray the same prayer, thinking your words will give you glory or a million dollars; God knows what you need from Him, so ask Him honestly (Matthew 6:7–8). After you ask honestly for what you need, then say the Lord's Prayer (check the King James Version; it may be getting corrupted in today's age) (Matthew 6:9–13). Love your neighbor and forgive them (Matthew 6:14–15). Do not lie for glory; hide righteousness away from vanity, and keep it to yourself (this doesn't mean don't love your neighbor just help them. Say you're welcome when they thank you, and move on to the next task) and God will reward thee (Matthew 6:16–18). Do not seek earthly possessions, seek that which is above (heaven) (Matthew 6:19–20; Colossians 3:1). Does your heart seek earthly or heavenly treasure? (Matthew 6:21). There is only one word that can define these verses; that word is *perceive,* and it's funny, the eye is the only part of our body that can perceive light from darkness (Matthew

6:22–23). Serve God and then you'll have no one to hate (Matthew 6:24). Don't worry about tomorrow; God is still providing for today (Matthew 6:25–26). You think, by your own hand, you can obtain anything? (Matthew 6:27) Fine clothes are still just body coverings (Matthew 6:28). Do not worry about that which you need; God knows what you need and will provide it (Matthew 6:30–32). Seek God, lawfulness, His righteousness, and from it, He will provide for you (Matthew 6:30). My favorite one: Worry only about what you have right in front of you today, because tomorrow will never be what you planned it to be (Matthew 6:34).

> Yesterday is history. Tomorrow is a mystery.
> Today is a gift. That's why it's called the present.
> (Master Oogway, *Kung Fu Panda*)

I would like to also say that praying, fasting, and alms are very well-linked together, and I would like to state again, when you do them, keep them a secret to yourself, seek no glory, just help when you can with what you can, and God will reward you. If someone doesn't understand it, help them out, and if you're praying together in church, that's not a bad thing. Just remember to keep it personal to you and those around you, and on a good occasion, do say a prayer for world peace (we do need it).

Now, I thought I would have an endless supply of things to say about prayers, but those things are nowhere to be found, so I'm gonna bring some Revelation in here. I have asked Christian after Christian this question, and not a one answered me honestly. I asked, "How will you buy what you and your family needs in the time of the great tribulation?"

They said, "What do you mean?"

I said, "According to the Book of Revelation, there will be an economy that, if you don't worship the beast and his image, you will not be able to purchase any provisions." (Revelation 13:17)

Then they jokingly said, "I will make what I need."

I said, "Really, you're gonna learn how to farm, preserve your seeds, preserve your food, hunt, make your own clothes, pay your taxes, and also provide for your family, all without electricity for seven years? Who's gonna teach you!"

This is where the two-by-four smacks them in the head because they, at this point, realize the convenience of modern living. A wise man once told me and a group of people that it's easy to say no to everything, but we need to come up with a solution. That's where rapture came in. I am a farmer, and I, only one year out of thirty, produce enough food for a year. I can't do it without both electricity and diesel fuel at this point. I was in that same boat. That's how I knew they couldn't answer the question. Many upon many think they will fight their way out, and to that I say, fight your way out of what? Who are you taking with you? And once out, how do you sustain? It hit me one day because of a book I read, and I will do a chapter on it, and I know it's probably gonna hurt my cause more than help it, but I am fearless on that subject. This is where the pre-rapture comes from; the fear of being here during the great tribulation. I have a good question for anyone leading the physical churches, and it goes, "What will you say to your congregation when we aren't raptured and they say, 'you said!'"

Let me tell you wisdom. A farmer once told me, when I was borrowing his equipment, "Do not fill that chopper box up on the first time, fill it one-tenth of the way full and empty it. Then fill it a quarter, half, three-quarters, and then full, and empty them and repeat this every day you use it." He gave to me a great life lesson that came from his farming, and it went like this. Expect that everything you do will fail and build up from there. So start with the expectation that your machines will fail, then you will not have to shovel out a full chopper box on the first go. There are a few references I can give you about rapture with regard to us still being here in that time. "The words of the blessing of Enoch, wherein he blessed the elect and righteous, who will be living in the day of tribulation. When all the wicked and godless are to be removed (Enoch 1:1). And the second reference is 1 Thessalonians 4:16–17. "For the Lord himself shall descend from heaven with a shout, with the voice of the archangel, and with the trump of God: and the dead in Christ shall rise first: then we which remain shall be caught up together with them in the clouds, to meet the Lord in the air: and so shall we ever be with the Lord."

This is a lot to take in, but the only time God shall descend from the heaven is (my favorite series of verses) Revelation 19:11–21.

> And I saw heaven opened, and behold a white horse; and he that sat upon him was called Faithful and True, and in righteousness he doth judge and make war. His eyes were as a flame of fire, and on his head were many crowns; and he had a name written, that no man knew, but he himself. And he was clothed with a vesture dipped in blood: and his name is called the Word of God. And the armies which were in heaven followed him upon white horses, clothed in fine linen, white and clean. And out of his mouth goeth a sharp sword, that with it he should smite the nations: and he shall rule them with a rod of iron: and he treadth the winepress of the fierceness and wrath of Almighty God. And he hath on his vesture and on his thigh a name written, KING OF KINGS, AND LORD OF LORDS. And I saw an angel standing in the sun; he cried with a loud voice, saying to all the fowls that fly in the midst of heaven, Come and gather yourselves together unto the supper of the great God; That ye may eat the flesh of kings, and the flesh of captains, and the flesh of horses, and of them that sit on them, and the flesh of all men, both free and bond, both small and great. And I saw the beast, and the kings of the earth, and their armies, gathered together to make war against him that sat on the horse, and against his army. And the beast was taken, and with him the false prophet that wrought miracles before him, with which he deceived them that had received the

mark of the beast, and them that worshipped his image. These both were cast alive into a lake of fire burning with brimstone. And the remnant were slain with the sword of him that sat upon the horse, which sword proceeded out his mouth: and all the fowls were filled with their flesh.

It continues in Revelation 20:1–6.

And I saw an angel come down from heaven, having the key of the bottomless pit and a great chain in his hand. And he laid hold of the dragon, that old serpent, which is the Devil, and Satan, and bound him a thousand years, and cast him into the bottomless pit, and shut him up, and set a seal upon him, that he should deceive the nations no more, till the thousand years should be fulfilled: and after that he must be loosed a little season. And I saw thrones, and they sat upon them, and judgment was given unto them: and I saw the souls of them that were beheaded for the witness of Jesus, and which had not worshipped the beast, neither his image, neither had received his mark upon their forehead, or in their hands; and they lived and reigned with Christ a thousand years. But the rest of the dead lived not again until the thousand years were finished. This is the first resurrection. Blessed and holy is he that hath part in the first resurrection: on such the second death hath no power, but they shall be priest of God and of Christ, and shall reign with him a thousand years.

This portion of Revelation 19 is very far into the great tribulation (or is this a combination of time periods of connected events?). And it is absolutely terrifying to read the events of tribulation. The word lives up to its meaning for sure. More on this is 2 Timothy 3:12–17.

> Yea, and all that will live godly in Christ Jesus shall suffer persecution. But evil men and seducers shall wax worse and worse, deceiving, and being deceived. But continue thou in the things which thou hast learned and hast been assured of, knowing of whom thou hast learned them; And that from a child thou hast known the Holy Scriptures, which are able to make thee wise unto salvation through faith which is in Christ Jesus. All scripture is given by inspiration of God, and is profitable for doctrine, for reproof, for correction, for instruction in righteousness: That the man of God may be perfect, thoroughly furnished unto all good works.

> I charge thee therefore before God, and the Lord Jesus Christ, who shall judge the quick and the dead at his appearing and his kingdom. (2 Timothy 4:1)

And Matthew 24:29–31:

> Immediately after the tribulation (begins or ends?) (after the four horsemen playing out or building up) of those days shall the sun be darkened (Revelation 16:10?), and the moon shall not give her light (Revelation 16:10?), and the stars shall fall from the heaven (Revelation 12:4?), and the powers of the heavens shall be shaken (Revelation 11:19?): and then shall appear the sign of the Son of man in heaven (this all sounds like Revelation chapter 12?): and then shall all the tribes of the earth morn, and they shall see

the Son of man coming in the clouds of heaven with power and great glory. And he shall send his angels with a great sound of a trumpet, and they shall gather together his elect from the four winds, from one end to the other. (Parentheses mine)

And Daniel 12:1–3:

And at that time shall Michael stand up, the great prince which standeth for the children of thy people: and there shall be a time of trouble, such as never was since there was a nation even to that same time: and at that time thy people shall be delivered (like how Jesus delivered the Jews?), every one that shall be found written in the book. And many of them that sleep in the dust of the earth shall awake, some to everlasting life, and some to shame and everlasting contempt. And they that be wise shall shine as the brightness of the firmament; and they that turn many to righteousness as the stars for ever and ever. (Parentheses mine)

And Revelation 3:10

Because thou hast kept the word of my patience (patience of the saints), I also will keep thee from the hour of temptation, (He will protect the righteous) which shall come upon all the world, to try them that dwell upon the earth. (Parentheses mine)

And Luke 21:32:

Verily I say unto you, this generation shall not pass away, till all be fulfilled.

And Luke 21:27–28:

> And then shall they see the Son of man coming in a cloud with power and great glory. And when these things begin to come to pass, then look up, and lift up your heads; for your redemption draweth nigh (if we are gone who will lift their head for redemption?). (Parentheses mine)

And Matthew 24:16–22:

> Then let them which be in Judaea flee into the mountains: Let him which is on the housetop not come down to take anything out of his house: Neither let him which is in the field return back to take his clothes. And woe unto them that are with child, and to them that give suck in those days! But pray ye that your flight be not in winter, neither on the sabbath day: For then shall be the great tribulation, such as was not since the beginning of the world to this time, no, nor ever shall be. And except those days should be shortened, there should be no flesh be saved: but for the elect's sake those days shall be shortened.

At this point, you might be asking who the elect are. I personally don't believe that they are the 144,000 chosen of the tribes of Israel (Jacob) because of 1 Peter 2:1–10. The most powerful one of these is the Book of Enoch, because he opened his book by addressing that very question: to pre-rapture or not to pre-rapture. If you don't yet believe in that series, it's OK. Answer me a question though, who made you personally reject it? (Maybe this rapture theory is the reason it was rejected. Weren't the Jews wanting a rapture from Jesus? Maybe they were still mad from that so they removed this book around 382 AD. No, I take that back. It was because Enoch prophesied about Jesus Christ and Jews do not like that, and that's 500 years before the flood prophecy that somehow survived the flood.) (It exists and it came from somewhere, did it not?)

And on the Bible side of my argument is 1 Thessalonians 4:16–17. This verse is for all the marbles, so I ask, "If we are raptured before Revelation 19, which is the end of the great suffering we call the great tribulation because the sinners are slain, who are the we which remain that will meet Him in the clouds and live with Him forever?" What these books are saying is we will be here. I know this great tribulation is a scary thing, but I'd like to try to settle your minds with that which you can do. Read 1 John chapter 4. The only answer I can find for this time is praying to the one being in the single spoken sentence (universe) who can actually deliver on those prayers. If you can love in the great tribulation more than yourself, how great is your love? To be starving, sick, beaten, persecuted, lied to, and dying and still show compassion, you will have done the very thing Jesus Himself was sent here to do (John 15:13). (Now you know why it must happen. The Jewish tradition doesn't accept Jesus, so they will suffer like He did. Then they will understand what His sacrifice truly meant. Christians, it's no different for you too. We are all going to know the pain we put Jesus through.)

Love. There will be days in the great tribulation where you get just enough, and days you will have to give all you have, and days you can't get but, rather, will have to help others do. That is assuming we can notice these things. Those are the days you will be tested, and your faith will be tested, and it will shine or fail to shine (Daniel 12:2).

A man told me, after a three-day power outage, that people were shoving and yelling at each other just for water at Walmart. How will we survive seven years? God and God alone will be your rock (water can come from that rock) (Exodus 17; Numbers 20).

"For it is written, a man doesn't live by bread alone, but by every word that proceedeth out of the mouth of God" (Matthew 4:4).

Would you choose to starve to death just to save a friend, family member, or a complete stranger just for a day, knowing he or she would die tomorrow? Jesus was so overtaken by the pending crucifixion when He prayed He was sweating blood (Luke 22:43–44). That's some real praying right there. I don't know exactly what's going to happen, but I do believe that suffering through the great tribulation is the way unto salvation, and I believe God will ease my days as much as He can, but I will pray to Him in all days, because my God is great (Psalms chapters 2, 3, 4, and 5). The "Key of Prayer" is that prayer is the only means of communication we have with our God; He may not speak in words, but His Words are the actions we are asking for. When the darkness comes, request a light. "Watch ye therefore, and pray always, that ye may be accounted worthy to escape all these things that shall come to pass, and to stand before the Son of man" (Luke 21:36).

The glimmer of hope. But of that day and that hour knoweth no man, no, not the angel which are in heaven, neither the Son, but the Father (Mark 13:32). This is what I believe this means: no one knows the day. Not even Jesus Christ knows the hour he shall descend, but when the Word is fulfilled by man's hand, then will come the day of the Lord. The glimmer being we, by our hand, can stop the second coming. Think about this; the devil can beat God, but it comes with a price. If the devil tries to defeat God, then by God's word shall he fall, but if he not deceive the nations, then the Word of God can never be fulfilled. His victory is at the price of submission to the will of God. Submit yourself, therefore, to God. He already told us who wins!

My belief? I do not believe in rapture. I would love to not be here in tribulation, but who will help those who say, "Lord, help me, Lord, send me a comforter?" Where will the comforters be? And who will be those who suffer and be captured for the Lord's sake? Who are those who deserve to live with the Lord forever after, meeting Him in the clouds? Who will be left to make the Jews jealous? (Romans 11:11). And finally, who will do the Lord's work during tribulation if Christians are gone? This is why the church is the assembly of Gods people. I don't know what's going to happen, and I'm not afraid to say it! But if I am here and you are here, and somehow, we meet or have to suffer together or never see each other, you have my prayers, and I hope I have yours. We will both need them greatly.

> But he that shall endure unto the end, the same shall be saved. (Matthew 24:13)

> He that overcometh shall inherit all things; and I will be his God, and he shall be my son. (Revelation 21:7)

CHAPTER 12

—— ⚭ ——

KEY OF FORGIVENESS

So now that I got you right where I want you, please allow me to tell you about the third and final foundation thought: forgiveness. This is what this key thing is all about. What good is God to His people, and the people to their God, if we can't be together? None that I can see, but thankfully, God has compassion, especially when Israel built that cow statue thingy. (They should have just looked up.) I have read Genesis more than any other book, and the main theme I keep coming across is that God creates, man screws it up, God judges, God gives man in accordance to what man deserves, man is stricken with grief, but then God always provides us with a means to be forgiven. Forgiveness is a very big deal, and I think this without a soft heart is impossible (anything regarding Paul and circumcision). Jesus gives you a soft heart, and it becomes completely possible.

OK, I'm gonna get a quick story in here. This is a big statement: one of the biggest blowouts of resentment I had was against my father. I was having trouble dealing with the running of his farm. It truly wasn't big enough for the both of us. I was so frustrated and angry that I cursed him out. It was a big fallout between us. That was the day my heart, soul, and body left that farm. It wasn't until a year was complete at my new farm that the truth was revealed to me. In my pursuit of answers within scriptures, I saw that a man must leave his old family and move on to seek that which he is looking for. After having seen and heard about the transfer of my father's place to him,

I realized that wouldn't have worked for me. I was sent out not by the interaction of me and my father but, rather, by God. He knew all that must come to be for that which I seek to come true. My entire life I was obsessed with farming, and He wanted what was best for me. It was hard to let go of that old farm, but because all that I have seen God do for me, my faith in God is strong.

At that time, I had hoped that my father would forgive me, but I never asked him, and I prayed that something would come to renew our relationship. Iris came to me first, and then came Liam. Before Liam came though, we had, and still have, a small deal running; I needed a place to put some animals, and he needed hay. It was funny how God pulled us back together even through this difficult time. And when Liam came, things began to get even better. I hope my father can forgive me for that blowout and for leaving the farm. It may be the only way he can be at peace. I don't know who will take over that farm when the time comes, but as I have stated, my tomorrow plans never work out, so I will handle it when confronted with that challenge, and I hope my father will come to this understanding and do the same.

Like I said, this was a big blowout of resentment, and because of it, I found the peace of mind, and it was in God's will for me to do. This portion of my life taught me a lot about forgiveness; how it is a push and a pull that connects people in an inseparable situation. When you wrong someone, you push, and when that screws them over, you have pulled, but when you ask someone, "Forgive me," you are pulling from them, and they will push you or forgive you; a response will be the needed separation of the situation (a close out or ending needed), but if the separation is not handled and left, the needed closure will grow into hatred, and it will be much harder to forgive. I think, on some level, me and my father sought forgiveness, even though neither of us had spoken it aloud (we are stubborn farmers). I may be talking from my butt here, but I don't think that deal would have happened so quickly if we each didn't want a way back into each other's life. And this deal has served both farms greatly over the last few years.

Forgiveness is a very powerful thing and it goes well beyond an "I'm sorry," right into the spirit. To seek a "forgive me, brother or sister" is no different than the seeking of forgiveness from God we so desperately need. This is why love hath no torment. When you are in love, not just with a spouse, but rather can show compassion to anyone where then can torment appear? (1 John 4). Forgiving is easy when you love, and love is better when you can forgive. Love becomes perfect, but when there is doubt, there is always torment. When there is no forgiveness, there is no love; therefore, I say to you, live well, laugh often, love much (Elisabeth-Anne "Bessie" Anderson Stanley).

The best fruits of life come from those who can forgive, and if a man or women cannot forgive, they do not give good fruits. Our differences, inexperience, selfishness, and lack of self-control are what drive doing the wrong thing to someone. Sometimes, it's better that we wrong someone and get an opportunity to humble ourselves (Proverbs 11:2). If you can rebuke someone who thinks wrongly, do it, but seek not his compliance. Let him renew his mind with the words you spoke, and if someone rebukes you, listen and take it with a grain of salt, but leave the chip at home, and when you get home, put the rebuke to the test and see if it holds up to scripture. Then your mind shall be renewed (Leviticus 19:17; Romans 12:1–2). I believe God has set us up to be continually in a state of wronging others, and then having to humble ourselves, and then having our minds renewed in order that we refine our beings and then we become upright (or maybe this is a condition of the first sin). Forgiveness is right smack dab in the middle of this process.

God's kingdom sounds like a rapture (look up the definition). With the world descending into darkness, it is easy for me to see that our beings will need much refining so that God's final kingdom can be flawless. By the time the people of God will get to heaven, they will know the weight their actions carry. The penalties all justify the actions, but for those that seek forgiveness for those wrong actions, their spiritual penalty shall be paid. Jesus did not come to destroy the law or take any law away He came to fulfill it (Matthew 5:17–20). And in that fulfilment, He can take away all your guilty verdicts from breaking the still-existing laws God would give you (no law, no guilt). So again, ask God and everyone you wronged for forgiveness, seek Him and everyone else out, and you shall be forgiven whether the humans say yay or nay (Matthew 5:37).

I would like to expand a little on the earlier portion about works, faith, and works of faith. Again, James said, "Faith, if it have not works, is dead." Jesus Christ is going to lift your guilt when you call upon him, and it is up to you to fill your life with good works from that calling on, because your works will be a reflection of your faith in Jesus Christ, and whether they be good or bad, you will be judged from thy works. Believe in Jesus's sacrifice, study Jesus's doctrine, live the life of Jesus as best you can, love your neighbors, and above all, *forgive and you shall be forgiven!* (Matthew 6:14).

OK, now, we will look at a narrative with regard to forgiveness in the Bible. In Genesis chapter 3, you're probably not going to understand the forgiveness portion (Genesis 3:19 foreshadowing his return) of Adam and Eve, because it's not in the Bible, but consider this; if God hadn't forgiven them on some level, why did God lift the curse of thorns after the flood? (Genesis 8:21), make them clothes to cover their shame, promise enmity between good and evil that they had now come to understand and more children who would sin and, in all seriousness, let us live after bringing death to His entire creation, and send His snake stomper, Jesus Christ.

Cain and Abel in Genesis chapter 4. Abel gave a good sacrifice, he essentially was forgiven by God, and then he died. Thankfully, God accepted his sacrifice. Then the Lord gave Cain, the man who killed Abel, a protection that no man can kill him without receiving sevenfold and again the ground curse lifted (Genesis 8:21) and more sinful children (not God's intent, of course). But importantly, God preserved Cain's line through Naamah and Noah (Seth and Cain's lines), a line that leads right to Jesus Christ. Then you got Genesis chapter 6, which has missing info everywhere. I'm not getting into that discussion here, but it ended in a flood, or did it?

Noah and his family were the only upright whom God allowed to live even though Noah became a drunkard and Ham (meaning literally "black") stole his father's clothes that he got from Adam (oops, I shouldn't have said that) and got a curse from his father that Ham/Canaan should be a servant to all others. They must have been forgiven, though, because all generations came from this event. And here is where the story of Genesis gets crazy—the tower of Babel. Let's face truth here, if the people who built the tower of Babel didn't get cursed to Babel, then they couldn't have babbled on (foreshadowing here). The people of the tower were scattered abroad, and James starts his book with, and to, those scattered abroad. Better than what happened to Sodom and Gomorra.

Genesis 6 and the story of the tower of Babel are very connected stories and are hard learned studies when you start digging into them. I believe the old evil made it through the flood in a new way. God must have forgiven on some level, because these were pretty dark days.

Let's go to Abraham now. The man who was promised the land of milk and honey, and an heir of God's kingdom, Jesus Christ. Abraham lied about who his wife was, which started some controversy, and he also didn't believe that God's promise was real in the sense that his wife and him arranged him to sleep with his servant. Ishmael came from this event, and there's a long interesting story behind that one. Then God has Abraham sacrifice his son, Isaac, stopping him at the last second and says, "Abraham, you have been faithful to Me." The Lord forgave the things Abraham did because of his faith in God. Check out Hebrews 11 again.

Then you have the sons of Isaac, who are Jacob and Esau. Jacob lied and deceived his blind father. He also, if I'm not mistaken, took four wives and only loved one of them. Then, having returned to his homeland, he demanded from God that God bless him (Jacob—he that wrestles with God). Here's where God forgave him. God passed the blessing of Abraham to Jacob, renamed him Israel (Israel—wrestles with God), and gave him the twelve tribes of Israel. And the blessing to Judah was Jesus Christ.

Now, Jacob loved his son, Joseph, more than the rest, and that's where we cross over into Exodus. At the end of Genesis, Joseph saves Egypt from a famine and becomes elevated by pharaoh and saves his brothers from starving to death. This is all after they sold him into slavery. God had a plan (Genesis 50:20). Exodus, as in the exodus of Israel. Israel had come under the command of a new and brutal pharaoh who sought to destroy Israel. So much so that he drowned all the baby boys of Israel. Thankfully, when Israel cried out to the Lord our God, Moses was saved by that pharaoh himself. If I'm not mistaken, Moses was elevated as a great commander of the Egyptians. God must have known this is what it would have taken to get His people out. And after God got his people out (great story), we come to Mount Sinai. So Moses is up on the mount and making a covenant with God so that Israel, through the teachings of the laws and God Himself's presents, can become a holy nation, and Israel crafts a cow to worship. Mind you that God, in the form of clouds and lighting, was right up on the mount (thanks, Aaron). Thankfully, though, Moses convinces God to forgive Israel because God wanted to destroy them.

And here's where Leviticus begins, because Moses, after building the tabernacle, could not enter (Leviticus 1:1). Leviticus is all about forgiveness, how people can become pure again, and then can live in God's presence. It's also what I consider the book of sacrifice. Keep in mind, though; something has to die in order for your sin to be lifted. That's why Jesus is so important (blood must be shed). He both beat the law by obeying it fully, in which death couldn't take Him by definition of the oldest law, and his physical death is now the blood that was needed to purify us, and when you partake in all He has asked of you, then you can receive Him as your atonement/ forgiveness. Leviticus had become corrupted and is easy to corrupt; that's why Jesus was sent. Jesus and His sacrifice cannot be corrupted. So it is to say, Leviticus was not made unlawful; Jesus was more pure for all peoples of the world to utilize as a savior.

Now, I will say this. God does not like death. He makes it clear in this book, so if you can be saved through Jesus and not have to sacrifice like in Leviticus to become pure and be subject to corruption, why wouldn't you spare the lives and believe in Jesus? O hear ye, Israel (Mark 12:28–33). Leviticus ends with the Lord talking to Moses in the tent (Leviticus 9:23), so he did become pure/forgiven by commandment of the Lord.

And now we're in Numbers. (We're cruisin' through forgiveness.) So Moses leads Israel to the Promised Land. This is a heart-breaking book, because both Moses and a generation disqualified themselves from ever seeing the Promised Land. This, after Moses again convinces God to spare them. Fool God once, He'll forgive you; try to do it again, and you're sentenced to wander in the desert for forty years and never get to see the Promised Land!

And then came the Levite rebellion. Things were not looking good. Then Moses, who was getting frustrated, hit the rock rather than commanding the rock and lost his own right to see the Promised Land. If things seem like they were getting dire, believe me, it gets worse. God curses Israel with venomous snakes, and once again, Moses has to beg God for forgiveness. (Moral here: Don't fool God. I hate snakes.) And not only did the snakes poison them, the snake was the cure by the commandment of the Lord.

Then we get to Moab. Balaam could not curse the people of God but only bless them. And what's even crazier, Balaam foretells of Jesus Christ. So now the children came forth to inherit the land. Deuteronomy begins as the teaching to this new generation who will inherit the Promised Land from Abraham's covenant with God. The Shema is very important to this portion of the Bible. It calls Israel to listen and to love the one true God with all your heart, soul, and might. You combine that with chapter 13, and you get one dead Jesus. (Sorry, that's a bad joke, but I am very serious, and if we can be forgiven for killing Jesus, that is a righteous God.)

Now, this book is, once again, teaching a new generation the same situation as in the Mount Sinai story. The new generation would have to deal with the people of Canaan. (I would like to know who, what, when, where, why, and how the idols, which are in the same manner as the books of Enoch, survived the flood and even how they survived from Babel, where all the knowledge of the world was written, and we were scattered everywhere in different languages so they couldn't understand that forsaken knowledge and how it made it to Babylon, which was raised and again made it all the way to today's day and age. Answer me this, scholars: how did idol worship survive the flood?)

Then, when you get farther into this book, it lays out social living and leadership qualities of leaders and worship. Boy, if we stuck to that, we would not have to ask for so much forgiveness. This is where that corruption I spoke of comes from—not listening to what God said is good to do. Moses ends the teaching by stating the choice is life or death, curse or blessing. He says, "Choose God," but then says, "When I die, I know you will not be faithful, but turn back to God, and he will give (circumcise) you(r) a new heart (Jesus Christ)." This is where the Torah ends, but we are going to continue to Jesus.

So Joshua is the lucky fella who led Israel into the Promised Land. It wasn't so easy, though; they meet the Canaanites, but thankfully, some were somewhat easier to convince God is God. And even when they got to the river and it was parted for them, they were meet with an angelic leader who had put them in their place. For he was with God, which begs the question, was Joshua really for God? Let's find out.

At the battle of Jericho the people of God listened to His commands, and by the commands, the walls of Jericho fell (walls work so good it takes God to bring them down. LOL. It's relevant to when I have lived). But an Israel man steals provisions from Jericho that belongs to God and lies about it, and the battle of Ai takes a turn. They got whooped. They had to repent and right the wrong and seek forgiveness in order that they could have victory. This was a lesson to Israel that, if they listen to God, they will defeat anything. They were great conquerors under God's command, and if you think this is violent, take a look at the Canaanites, but remember what I first said. Some Canaanites changed to believe in the one true God. God forgave the Canaanites (where do you think convert or die came from? it comes from the book of Joshua). Joshua then divided the lands and gave his final speeches about being faithful to the covenant.

Judges is probably Israel at its worst. (Don't hold me to that.) The Canaanites that stuck to their idol worship were not dealt with as God commanded, which I know would have been genocide if there weren't Canaanites that switched sides, but the failure to get rid of them morally corrupted Israel. (Thankfully though, Simon was on our side.) It becomes a never-ending cycle of evil, violent leadership, and idol worship, and it gets worse and worse faster and faster. And if you think for a second, Samson was a great hero of Israel. He was, by far, the worst of the leaders. Even though God had given strength to these not so good leaders, what would you do in His shoes? *Save the people!* God worked with what he had available.

Judges 21:25 sums up this period of time. I wish there were forgiveness in here, but I think it ended with a civil war. If I could sum this up, you turn from God, your destruction is certain. You obey God, your life is guaranteed.

Then we got a book of Ruth, which is from when the judges ruled. A woman who was very upright and very loyal ends up marring a respectable man. So in the days of the judges, you had people who were still righteous. This book sheds a little light on why God didn't destroy Israel. (There were people worth saving, and He will not destroy a one.) That was a story of forgiveness, because Naomi and Ruth found mercy from God in their relative, Boaz. So 1 Samuel starts with a woman, Hannah, who cannot have children, but after fasting, praying, weeping, becoming humble to the Lord, and vowing the child would serve, the Lord God gave her a man child, Samuel the prophet.

I am assuming now that, after the civil war somehow, all or a great sum of Israel united to fight back the Philistines, and the only way they could do it is by uniting. (Seems to be a common theme in historical war movies.) Some Israelites, thinking that God would handle the Philistines, marched the Ark of the Covenant out. (Forgive them, they had just come out of a civil war. They may not have known much about the ark.) And why would God help them? They had just gone into a civil war amongst themselves. Why? Because God loves His people, so after the Ark is stolen, God, without an army, smites the Philistines with plagues, and the Philistines sent it back. Then the humbled Israel goes to Samuel and says, "Find us a king."

Samuel goes to God, and God says, "Yeah, it's probably a bad idea, but if the people want one, give them one." So enter Saul, which is funny, because he was just like Hitler—full of promise, and then he just flipped the switch. Dishonest, couldn't see past himself, and disobedient to God.

Samuel confronts him and says, "Hey, you're supposed to be humble and obedient, and because of the things you have done, you're gonna get replaced."

So cue David, a young boy with an unwavering faith in God. (We'll see if that holds up.) Here is a young boy like Joshua. He could defeat anything because he believed so much in God, and he was humble. Saul was pretty mad about being replaced, and he hunted and sought to kill David after David was becoming beloved by many from his victories (David—beloved). David's humble nature is shown in the opportunities he had to kill Saul, and he chooses not to. I have gone a little while without saying forgiveness in this chapter of forgiveness, but here it comes. David and Saul's inner wars run through later 1 Samuel. David has an opportunity to kill Saul, but he did not. One of my favorites is when David cuts off the cloth, and Saul says, "David, thou art more righteous than I, for thou hast rewarded me good, whereas I have rewarded thee evil. And thou hast shewed this day. How that thou hast dealt well with me, forasmuch as when the LORD had delivered me into thine hand, thou killest me not. For if a man find his enemy, will he let him go well away? Wherefore the LORD reward thee good for that thou hast done unto me this day. And now, behold, I know well that thou shalt surely be king, and that the kingdom of Israel shall be established in thine hand."

Then David swears not to kill Saul's line. If you didn't catch this, this is what stubborn forgiveness looks like. The higher power, who is God, had brought those two men to an inseparable situation, and Saul, being humbled by David's guilt, gave David his unofficial blessing for kingship, and in return, David forgave Saul and didn't pursue killing off the line of Saul. Unfortunately, you only get so many chances at forgiveness before God acts, and Saul and his sons were destroyed in the war against the Philistines.

2 Samuel. So it opens with the lamentations of David of Saul's death (*Wow!* A book of Jasher reference. Where did that come from?) (2 Samuel 1:18). So this humbling of David brings him to kingship after a short conquering of the tribes (more to unify rather than to destroy). Then, when David wants to build God a temple to worship Him, God says He'll build one for David, and out of it will come Jesus Christ. So now comes David's fall, because, wouldn't you know it, we all fall short. He sees a women bathing on a roof, and he inquires about her and gets her pregnant. Then he brought the

wrath of God down on himself by having her husband assassinated in battle so he could have her as his wife. This was a fatal mistake on many counts.

God Himself says, "I have provided wives for you, yet you do this evil?" (paraphrased). So after getting called out on his mistake, David enters a time of repentance/forgiveness seeking and serious repentance, but the damage was done. David came out of his humble nature, and because of it, his kingdom fell apart. This is the weight of evil actions. The woman who he had taken, her son became the heir. So here we go again, a repeat of an older chapter, Judges.

1–2 Kings. I mean, it is a mirror image of Judges. You want to know where poly tics came from, read these books. And for those of you that think Sumerians were some ancient alien nonsense, you need to pay attention to their timeline. There is a resurgence of Sumeria within the northern kingdom of Israel (watch for things that keep coming back). The only importance the nonexistent dimension of time has is to show where you are. The past is history, and it must line up, and the future is set by the Word of God. Sorry, Father-in-law, but math can only predict where something will be and confirm where it was, but try letting math express the now (that would be sorcery). That's math's only function, and it's tied to three parameters. Distance between point a and b and velocity, the rate at which it travels, and energy, how much of something hidden it took to produce motion, but motion is dependent upon the distance something traveled, and the velocity it traveled at is dependent upon the applied energy needed to move. The riddle is who set it in motion? Time is only the perception of motion, and the flaw in mathematical equations and our time is running out. (How would you measure time without motion?)

Man, now I see what that liar and thief Einstein was going through eight hours of writing on four hours of sleep. I'm getting delusional. OK, I've rested and let's get back to Solomon and 1–2 Kings. This is where the final straw of God's patience gets tested because this short downfall leads us right to Babylon. *Literally.* So Solomon, man, that guy had a lot of wives, but he married for alliance rather than love. Don't let politics run (and ruin) your life. It wasn't long into Solomon's rein that he partook in idol worship. Then, after Solomon was the kingdom of Israel. Israel was split, and eventually, they both fell to unrighteousness. Then came the prophets. I could make this book go on forever with regard to forgiveness, but we're gonna stick to the timeline and heading to Jesus. The northern kingdom did not heed the words of the prophets and was conquered by Syria. The southern, however, is an interesting story. Josiah found a book called the book of law. (Wonder what books were included in that canon.) But it was that book that turned that whole kingdom on its head. They immediately reformed, but it was too late. (That's both a powerful book, and reformers now have nothing on the righteousness of that book. Keep reforming though; we all need it.) Israel was taken to Babylon. I don't know if it was all of them, and you will have to piece the remainder together with the remaining books of the Old Testament. There is not much time though between Israel's capture and its return. Maybe a little less than a hundred years. Again, a historian may be able to shed more light on this. Daniel predicts the next 500–600 years up to Jesus, and I'm gonna be honest, not much in the Biblical sense is going on (or is there). Daniel talks about a great statue that would be destroyed by a rock with the head of gold (Babylon), the breast of silver (Medo Persia), the thighs of brass (Greece), the legs of iron (Romans), and the feet of iron and clay.

Now, the feet are the current world and not as important to this narrative, but these are the kingdoms that came and went during this time. Many wars and much suffering and idol worship had led the world into the best ever time for the ultimate act of forgiveness to take place. Jesus is born in the midst of the Roman Empire. He was the rock that destroyed the statue in the vision and created a broken semi-strong world where the clay is as powerful as the iron (broken in the sense that all are of equal stature, making it very difficult to wage war, the same as this era in time). This era, these wars, and this suffering were a small portion of why the people overlooked there savior. They thought he had come to deliver Israel from the Romans, but they did not understand that He did. The death that comes from the sin of this world had been defeated, and an advocate with the Father rose on the third day, and even the Roman Empire collapsed on itself because of its lawlessness. The clay had had enough, and the clay and iron were now equal and mixed.

Now, let's finish this saga here with the last days of Jesus. The corrupted Pharisees had gotten the people of God stirred up. The people had revolted because of the things Jesus was doing, saying, and teaching, because they didn't understand them. Let me put it to you this way: Jesus Himself tells Nicodemus, "How can you begin to understand that which is spiritual when you can't even understand that which is earthly?"

Then Pontius Pilot is like, "I have to act or I will lose those provinces to riots." So he arrests Jesus with no conviction to put upon Him. Then he says, "Whom will you Jews/Israelites have me save? This guilty man, or your Lord and Savior?"

The Jews did not pick the king of the Jews, Jesus. They condemned Him to death, and they are the one who said crucify Him. Then Pontius says, "I wash my hands of this." (He knew exactly who and what Jesus is and was and wanted no part in His death.)

When Jesus died up on the cross, a couple things happened; Jesus forgave one last man. Jesus said, "Forgive them, for they know not what they do." (This is the ultimate signifier that Jesus loved His neighbors as Himself.)

The saints arose, there was a great earthquake, and the Romans said, "Oh my god, we have killed the Son of God." The Romans believed in Jesus Christ more than the people who wrestle with God through this entire story, because they sent Jesus to the grave with armed guards to watch the grave so no man deceived the Jews. When in all history has a man like Jesus ever been sent dead to the grave with an armed escort? And on the third day, another great earthquake struck again, and an angel rolled back the door. After the guards saw these events, they ran to the Pharisees, arms and all. And we all know what happens next. (I'm not going to reference any of this narrative. I kept it as close to the topic of forgiveness as I could. Please make a determination of your own accord and your own studies and, as always, test mine.)

My conclusion is that this entire Bible thing is to teach us one thing: That we all can be forgiven! You would think that God would just give up on us, but He is truly slow to anger.

The key of forgiveness is that you have until you are dead to receive it, but don't think for a second you can wait and get to it later; God will come like a thief in the night to both the forgiver and the unforgiver. Get it done and done right.

CHAPTER 13

KEY OF ME

So let me start off by stating I didn't want any other of my keys on chapter 13 so they wouldn't be discredited. I know how the Hebrews are very big on their numbers, and I know the skepticism that comes from 13, but hey, if it weren't for bad luck, I wouldn't have any luck. This will be a short chapter.

So I've shared a little of my life with you, and it has been best summed up by a verse from a song written by Leonard Cohen. "It's a cold and it's a broken Hallelujah." What I mean to say is it has had its fair share of longsuffering. Thankfully, that is the way to (of) the Lord. Patience, longsuffering, and mercy. It has been a blessing, though, and writing this book has been awesome. Know this, though; this is how I currently view that which I spoke of. It is subject to change at a moment's notice. I like talking and even nonviolently arguing with people, especially about God. I think He needs our help and we all should give it in any capacity we can.

I want to do another quick little exercise with paper and pen. Put your name and the name of everyone you know who is Christian around the word *Bible,* which should be put in the center of the page. Also put circles around the words and draw a line from the names to the Bible circle. This is how I entered Christianity. I thought that it took what everyone knows about the Bible to crack the Bible's mysteries, and the more people you throw at the Bible, the more it could be understood.

This is how Christianity really works. Turn the page over, put your name in the center of the page, and draw a circle around it. Now, randomly put every name of every book on the remaining portion of the page. There are sixty-six of them, so be conservative with space. Now, draw a line from the books to your name. The books themselves can stand alone in your faith, and they will shape your faith. Now, draw a line between the books if you can. Each one of these books is a key to the levels of coding in which the Bible is written, yet you could strip the book down to a single word, "thee," and God would still be the definite article. In order to bolster your faith, you will have to read it. We all are deceived and need to listen.

Now, each book of the Bible does unlock another portion of itself, but it's the code the Bible is written in that truly blows my mind. (I will admit, I don't think I've read all the books of the Bible, and I definitely can't direct quote it.) It is written in truth. It is spiritually, physically, and metaphorically true. A good one from Kent Hovind is *Basic Instruction Before Leaving Earth*. Like I said, I don't know what is going to happen, and I barely understand the time I live in, but this I know: Jesus is the king, Jesus is my savior, Jesus died for my sin, Jesus will intercede at my judgment, Jesus inherits the throne of God, because Jesus is God.

Now, I would just like to say, if you know me, please do not hold me any higher than the man I am. I wrote this book because of the life I lived after I sought out the Lord and had put truth to my life. So please don't seek me out with the intent to harass me. Come meet me and share your story with me; the door is always open.

Also, I didn't really write this book for all people, though I will be blessed if it makes it out to people. I still haven't figured out how to get it out yet. I wrote it for my family, for they who had led me to God are now descending into darkness. God is sending one of His glimmers of hope. The key of me is the same as the key of you, which is to say, we need to wake up from our nightmare and listen, and if you listen close enough, you will hear the voice of God in your life.

Side note about me: I have come to desire the reproving of my faith because it has become stronger when my errors are pointed out. I may not always agree or take your side in that moment, but your dedication to your faith will also, in a moment, reprove mine. When I hear things, when my mind accepts them by resolution of testing, they do appear in my belief and speaking, and it is both amazing and a wonder of faith. You would think it would be possible to come to understand everything, but in a second, I've been proven so wrong. Faith has been, to me, a never-ending progression of understanding. That is a real mystery: how God could create such a thing. That's real power to create the thoughts themselves.

Want to know yourself? Track morals to their origin.

CHAPTER 14

KEY OF THE DEDICATED MAN

So here it comes, the chapter that will take everything I got to write, and it may not sit well with many Christians, but I'm writing it nonetheless because of two reasons. First, it set me straight. Second, the Bible without it was out of place for me, but the Bible was not without its ability to save me and also you. (I promise I will explain what this means.) If you didn't catch that, you don't have to read the books of Enoch to be saved. Nobody has presented it to me as a book I have to read or else, and I'm not saying that to you. (Choose to read or not to read for yourself, please.) It's not that kind of book. It is a book that will put all things in their place and, in so doing, immerses you to the true world you live in. Before I read this book, I thought the world ain't so bad. Then I read the book and was horrified. I believe God Himself sent me through these books to straighten me out. When I was a boy, I watched *Hercules* by Disney. I was fascinated with the Greek gods and goddesses, but it wasn't 'til right before I called Jesus that I rekindled the great search. The great search for me was trying to discover the truth behind where all the fables like the Greek gods and goddesses originated. It definitely found me. And don't think I don't know about 2 Timothy 4:4. God was very determined to both explain where they came from and terminate my fascination to them. They all originated about the span of five hundred years before the flood. Probably a little longer than that, but I don't think by much.

In this chapter, I will go through the entire book and make comparisons and give brief notes. I assure you I will try not to make it as long as the books themselves, but it will take a little bit to get through. I want to state here and now that this book doesn't ask you to believe in anything different than what the Bible already teaches, and Jesus is very much in this book series. I personally believe Jesus in these books is why they were cast out of the Biblical canon we refer to as the Bible.

Again, this chapter is up to you personally, whether or not you want to go through it. If not, skip it please!

I want to perplex you with a question. What are these verses talking about? Genesis 6; Ephesians 6:12; 1 Timothy 4:1; James 2:19; the whole Matthew 8 demon thing with Jesus; Matthew 25:41; 1 Corinthians 10:20–21; Psalms 106:37–38; Ephesians 6:10–12; Acts 19:13–16; 2 Peter 2:4–10; Revelation 9:1–7; Jude 1:6, 14–15; and 1 Peter 3:17–20. These are just some of things that make it sounds like there is a whole other world out there.

These are hard to explain, considering Jesus Himself said to Nicodemus, "How can you, Nicodemus, even begin to understand the spiritual when you can't even understand the earthly?" (John chapter 3). (Well not all of them.) Where is the prophecy of Enoch? (Jude 1:14). So let's talk about Enoch of Seth's line and see what the Bible says about him.

Enoch dedicated:

- Genesis chapter 5
- 1 Chronicles chapter 1
- Luke chapter 3
- Hebrews chapter 11
- Jude chapter 1

Not too much, but he's in there, and I'm not sure why his name is spelled Henoch in Chronicles. Here is the mind bender, because this topic goes so much deeper; Jesus Christ and others taught from this book of Enoch (again, I will explain), and he was taken by God. What does that mean? I know this because some of the teachings of Jesus seem completely new when He speaks them, because they first appear in the Bible when He speaks them in the new testimony. Would God have kept those teachings a secret from Israel so Jesus could give the Gentiles a one-up on the Jews? The answer is no; it is because the teaching no longer exist in the Bible canon. It may or may not have been taken out late in third century AD, because religious leaders didn't like the imagery that book came with. Who are they, and who is anyone who says that scriptures are limited to what exists in the current Bible? How many bibles are there, and what percent must be *different* to acquire a patent? And why is there a movement right now to *remove* the book of Revelation? Cursed be he who does that?

The strongest case I can bring forth with Jesus's teachings was the one about whose wife will she be. That teaching about angels did not come new; it was already taught. And also, where did the Jude 1:6 teaching come from. What scripture did we err by not knowing.

Before I state this, I would like to again state and pray that I get this chapter right, so God, please let me see again the things I need to see so I may speak all that must be spoken so I help, in any sort of way, at least one individual who is stuck like I was stuck. Please, God, help them find what they are looking for like how You have helped me find what I was looking for.

This is your third and final warning. If you do not read the books of Enoch and this chapter, you have no reason to hate me for writing this. If you are Christian and read this, by the second law, you really have no right to hate me, period, and if you are not Christian and just reading this chapter and that book, you will be confused. Be patient; this is the second time I have read the books of Enoch, and my patience was spent in the five years I was studying the current Biblical canon. If you choose not to read these books and skip this chapter, it is OK. I will not be mad at you and hold a grudge against you. Christianity is a journey, and all of our journeys are different.

Books of Enoch Derived from the R.H. Charles Translation, 1917

The book of the prophet, or the first book of Enoch

- Chapter 1:1—again, this book opens as a blessing to the generation who will be living in the tribulation (Matthew 24:13; 1 Thessalonians 4:16).
- Chapter 1:2–10—Enoch is declaring that God will descend from heaven, and all will tremble (James 2:19; Psalms chapter 68; Revelations chapter 19).
- Chapter 1:11–14—the righteous and elect are two different things, but they will be protected (Proverbs 2:6–11; Revelations 3:10, 9:4).
- Chapter 1:15–17—(Psalm 68:17; Revelation 19)
- Chapter 2 to chapter 5:3—all things are held in place and done by the Word of God and do not transgress that word.
- Chapter 5:4–10—the hardhearted do not the command of the Lord. This is why getting rid of the stone heart is very important.
- Chapter 5:11–12—forgiveness shall be given to them that rejoice (Romans 12:15; Psalms 135:3).
- Chapter 5:13—the law of sin and death or the curse of death by sin
- Chapter 5:14–19—(Matthew 5:5; Proverbs 9:10; Ephesians 4:2; James 4:6; Revelation 20:4)
- Chapter 6—this is crossing into Genesis 6 in the days of Jared, who is Enoch's father. The fallen angels who became the watchers planned a great sinful act.
- Chapter 7—the watchers each took a wife to bear fruit. The result was 11,250 foot tall giants (approximate height unless I got my units of measurement wrong) that ate everything, and the women became acquainted with root cutting, charms, enchantments, and herbs.
- Chapter 8—Azazel taught how to make war gear, working metals, the use of silver, and beautification, and from

this alone arose much godlessness and fornication. Also taught by others was root cutting, enchantments, resolving enchantments, astrology, constellations, signs of the earth, signs of the sun, course of the moon, and as men perished, their cry went up to heaven.

- Chapter 9:1–5—our cries made it to four high angels of the Lord, and we humans brought suit against the watchers.
- Chapter 9:6—this is a very important verse. Because we did not strive to learn the things, we did not get all that comes with strife. We did not obtain pure knowledge. This knowledge is corrupted (Ecclesiastes 1:17–18).
- Chapter 9:7–10—pleading our case.
- Chapter 10:13—Uriel is dispatched to Noah to help him prepare for the flood.
- Chapter 10:4–7—Raphael is dispatched to bind Azazel 'til he will be thrown into the lake of fire.
- Chapter 10:8–10—Gabriel is dispatched to set the giants against themselves so they may kill themselves off before the flood.
- Chapter 10:11—Michael's dispatched to bind all the watchers.
- Chapter 10:12—the fallen angels become watchers because they have to witness their sons destroy themselves, and the watchers are bound for seventy generations until they are to be cast into a lake of fire (Jude 1:6). That is very important because, from the seventh man Enoch to Jesus Christ, there are seventy generations.
- 10:13–14—all evil in all generations will be bound to the penalty the watchers shall pay. I wonder, though, if that is happening now, and if the abyss of fire is the same as the lake (Revelation chapter 20).
- 10:15–22—foreshadowing the events up to and after Noah's flood event and also states the curse of the earth not producing to her full yield will be lifted (verse 19 = Genesis 8:21) (Revelation 9:1–7).
- Chapter 11—a good bit of blessings.

- Chapter 12—Enoch who, at this time, was with the holy ones, was dispatched to reprimand the watchers. Here's a perplexing point to bring up. No man hath seen God(John 1:18). "Enoch walked with God: and he was not; for God took him" (Genesis 5:24). How does a man who was taken by God not see God? Maybe he really did became an angel who leads all other angels (that was a Metatron reference, and it's not really a supernatural thing).
- Chapter 13:1–3—Enoch speaks to the watchers, and they are stricken with fear.
- Chapter 4–10—the watchers ask Enoch to write up a petition, for the watchers sought forgiveness. Enoch has a dream and explains it to the watchers.
- Chapter 11–25—Enoch recaps his vision to the watchers and tells them their petition will not be granted. I'm pretty sure Enoch met Jesus (maybe), although he was not able to behold Him and neither were the angels.
- Chapter 15–1—he then sat and called to Enoch and said, "Fear not righteous man, scribe of righteousness, hear my words to say to the watchers, 'You should intercede for men, not men for you.'" That is very important because this leads into:
- Chapter 3–6—These are the lessons Jesus Christ taught.
  - Matthew 22:28–30—Jesus said she would be no man's wife when she dies. He said you do err by not knowing the scriptures. (What scriptures are those?) When we are resurrected, we are as the angels of God in heaven. And when we become spiritual, we cannot take wives lest we be defiled with the blood of women and bear giants again. We will be spiritual living in heaven with God and immortal; what more could we want as the ministering angels? If you don't believe me, it's OK. I'm not gonna take it personally, but you may want to consider these parables about the man who planted a fig tree that bore no fruit and cut it down. That was a reference to what would happen to

those that would produce no faith. And the one about the man who sent his only son to the vineyard to collect the fruit from the husbandmen. That was a reference to every time God made amends with men, even to the point that Jesus, God's Son, was sent. These are just a couple of the deep-rooted teachings, and those teachings are much older than we think.

- Chapter 8–11—this is the explanation of the demons. They are stuck here on earth because they were not produced by God, who produced His creation with spiritual origin. That which was produced of spiritual origin will return to the spiritual place, and that with earthly origin shall remain on earth. And they are nothing but violence, because they have no spirit by God. They are completely taken by the lust of the flesh. And their spirits shall rise up against man because we made them as our flesh has risen up against our Father (John 3:13).

- Chapter 16:1–2—and the spirits of these demons shall destroy until the day of tribulation, because they cannot be judged; they cannot leave the earth. This is why the earth must be destroyed—to destroy the demons that are bound to it (Revelation 20; Revelation 21:1).

- Chapter 3–5—God has Enoch declare unto the watchers that they had hard hearts, they know worthless knowledge, and they would have no peace.

- Chapter 17—Enoch is moving through places (he does this a lot). It's interesting, though, the part about the bow and the sword.

- Chapter 18:1–10—Enoch is moving through the heavens, I believe. Important note: the corner stone of earth (Job 38:6). The four winds (Revelation 7:1).

- Chapter 11–15—is describing the prison of stars and hosts of heaven. Even they are held to the commandments of God.

- Chapter 19—Uriel declares that the angels that connect with women will stand in this place. Women, you have it much harder than men, and you need to be faithful to the Word of God like Ruth was (loyal) because of Ecclesiastes chapter 7. Go to Genesis 3:16. And men, chapter 17, 18, and 19 in order. We both shall receive the kingdom of God (sorry for the detour).

- ○ This is the first declaration of idol worship. And the spirits of those angels shall also stand in this place until judgment.
- ○ Women who went astray with these angels become sirens.
- ○ This is important to me because I am not trying to be an Enoch. I am trying to describe, in my own words, with my own heart, what the books of Enoch have taught to me. I can barely imagine the things he is describing.

- Chapter 20—Uriel watches Tartarus, Raphael watches over the spirit of men, Raguel enforces the world of the luminaries, Michael is set over the best part of mankind and over chaos, Saraqael is set over the spirits whom sin in the spirit, Gabriel is set over the Paradise and the serpents, and the cherubim Remiel is set over those who rise.
- Chapter 21—Enoch describes in more detail the prison of the angels. It's funny; there are seven stars, and the seven stars of revelation are angels, and the seven churches have some problems. I wonder if they are connected.
- Chapter 22:1–5—the place we go when we die and await the day of judgement.
- Chapter 6–9—the breathing spirit of Abel continues to make suit against his brother, Cain.
- Chapter 10–17—three places: one for righteous spirits, one for sinners, and one for those who seek vengeance against sinners that will not perish nor can rise (vengeance is not mine, so saith the Raphael) (Hebrews 12:24).
- Chapter 23—wow, the luminaries have a harasser too, like we have the devil harassing us.
- Chapter 24—I believe, at this point, Enoch was entering where God Himself resides and keeps his tree of life.

- Chapter 25:1–2—Enoch declares he wishes to know all things (man before my own heart! Think about it).
- Chapter 25:3—the throne and says God will come down with goodness (that's a reference to Jesus Christ's coming, the first one in which He alone gave us eternal life).
- Chapter 25:4—no one can touch the tree, though, until the great judgment and the removal of the unlawful.
- Chapter 25:5—it shall be given to the righteous and holy, and fruit for the elect. Big separation of righteous, holy, and the elect.
- Chapter 25:6–9—more wonderful blessings.
- Chapter 26—Enoch sees some things. Trees in the middle of the earth? Daniel chapter 4?
- Chapter 27—Uriel explains the place. I'm not sure what it is, though. Sounds like a place of judgment.
- Chapter 29–31—Enoch is seeing places and describing them.
- Chapter 32—Enoch sees the garden of righteousness and the tree of wisdom Adam and Eve ate from. (Genesis 3).
- Chapter 33—Enoch references when he wrote the book of luminaries.
- Chapter 34—Enoch describes the northern portals; one is good, but the other two are violent and bring cold.
- Chapter 35—he doesn't say much about the west and the east portals.
- Chapter 36—southern portals bring warmth. Also, there are another series of portals for the stars in the sky.

The Parables: First

- Chapter 37—Enoch declares the book is for the men of old (guess that makes me a man of old), but it's not withheld from anyone, and the Lord of spirits gave Enoch this wisdom to write about in vison (Proverbs 9:10).
- Chapter 38—(Revelation 19)
- Chapter 39—and it also describes the dwelling place of the holy and the resting place of the righteous (Revelation 14:1–

5). And I think Jesus was there. Verse 20 is interesting. "Holy, holy, holy, is the Lord of Spirits that filleth the earth with spirits (Isaiah 6:3). Holy, holy, holy, is the Lord of hosts: his glory fills the whole earth (Revelation 4:8). Holy, holy, holy Lord God Almighty, which was, and is, and is to come.

- Chapter 40:1—again, thousands of thousands and ten thousand times ten thousand.
- Chapter 40:2—those that sleep not are (Revelation 4:8).
- Chapter 40:3–15—explanations of the four presences. Also, further descriptions of the angels Michael, Raphael, Gabriel, Phanuel. Michael, though, is, important to note, merciful and longsuffering. There couldn't be two better words to place next to each other (Exodus 34:6; Psalms 86:15; Romans 2:4; Joel 2:13).
- Chapter 41:1—wow to this one (Matthew 5:17–19).
- Chapter 41:2—and this one too (John 14:1–4).
- Chapter 41:3–14—again, Enoch is giving knowledge regarding the luminaries and also again states that they don't transgress the commands of God, and he goes further by saying not even the angels can hinder the strengthening of the righteous through Jesus Christ (Mark 7:18–20).
- Chapter 42—wisdom is deep seated in the heavenly, not the earthly (John 3:11–12)
- Chapter 43:1—(Psalms 147:4)
- Chapter 43:2—other lightning and stars that shine by their righteousness.
- Chapter 43:3—great science.
- Chapter 43:4–7—those other lightning and stars are us, so shine bright, brothers and sisters (Daniel 12:3).
- Chapter 44—become a new creature (2 Corinthians 5:17)

The Parables: Second

- Chapter 45—beware ye sinners, there is nothing good that will happen to you. Again, Jesus is all over this chapter (Revelation 21:1).

- Chapter 46:1–2—the second coming.
- Chapter 46:13—(Matthew 19:23–24).
- Chapter 46:14—Idol worshippers.
- Chapter 46:15—(2 Timothy 3:12)
- Chapter 47—(Revelation 6:10)
- Chapter 48:1–2—(Proverbs 14:27)
- Chapter 48:3–4—the Son of Man is named.
- Chapter 48:5–6—(John 1:1–2)
- Chapter 48:6—(Psalms 23:4)
- Chapter 48:7—(Luke 2:32)
- Chapter 48:8—(Romans 14:11)
- Chapter 48:9—these were Jesus's purposes.
- Chapter 48:10–12—God perseveres the lot of righteous through the Christ. Immanuel—God is with us, and when you take up His name, God is with you (Acts 4:12).
- Chapter 48:13–15b—(Psalms 2:1–10)
- Chapter 48:16–21—(Isaiah 42)
- Chapter 49:1–6—Jesus will come and pour out wisdom to a generation that has fallen asleep.
- Chapter 48:7–8—verse 7 is really important because of Mark 12:28–34 and other instances such as this. Jesus speaks as one with authority and can never be rebuked because His wisdom is always truth.
- Chapter 50:1–3—(Revelation 20:6)
- Chapter 50:4–10—(Revelation 20:11–15; Revelation 2:22)
- Chapter 51:1–2—(Revelation 20:13)
- Chapter 51:3–5—(Revelation 20:4).
- Chapter 51:6–9—sounds like a good day to me.
- Chapter 52—this is a hard one for me. I think two thoughts on this one. First, it sounds much like that statue of Daniel's book in the empire of clay and iron mixed. It's very difficult to wage war. The second is God will make acquisition of materials impossible like Revelation 13:17.
- Chapter 53—idol worship, lawlessness in the valley (I think it's obvious which valley), angels prepare for war. And the righteous shall have rest (Revelation 19).

- Chapter 54—Enoch is talking about the valley the watchers are to be held in and how. Verse 5 has some old Greek references on how the gods arose and the titans fell. Old stuff. Again, he references the coming flood.

OK, now time to take a break. We are halfway there. I had to stop many times through this. My head hurt writing and referencing this. I want to take this moment to bring in a thought here. This is something I haven't quite figured out yet. Revelation is a twisted mess. A lot of people think that the thousand-year age is coming still. I'm not fully sold yet. I just haven't unraveled it yet because of this verse by Peter: 2 Peter 3:1–8 and 13.

Where do I even begin? First, the thousand-year kingdom as a day, and a day as a thousand-year kingdom? Secondly, the flood that destroyed the old world, and the heavens and earth which are now. This is interesting. "And I saw a new heaven and a new earth: for the first heaven and the first earth were passed away: and there was no more sea" (Revelation 21:1). Boy, that sounds like the flood to me. The ignorant are looking for and waiting for something that already exists.

I think I finally settled this in my mind. Let me try yours: How many castings in the lake of fire shall there be? I answer one in which all will be tried before the Lord of Hosts and given in accordance to the life they have lived, whether it be righteous or unrighteous, and on that day of days shall all wickedness be cast into the second death. So if my theory is true, there will come the last battle in which the devil, having had been released from prison to deceive, will rise up and Jesus, with His army, shall descend down to conquer the devil and then judge all. I say this because Revelation is just like the book of Enoch in that they both are switching between periods of time and also are jumping back and forth through time all over the place. The time of the seventieth generation and the time of the end battle Armageddon are two good focus points for this discussion. So then the abyss of fire is different than the lake of fire, and also, things within Revelations could have already happened. (Abyss is just a holding cell, and the lake is the literal end.) I believe this because many fulfillments happened when Jesus Christ of Nazareth came for the first time. And also if, and this is a big if, the book of Enoch is correct, then all the watchers are now in the abyss of fire. So when that angel came down to release Jesus from the tomb, the angel or another one may have brought the devil to the bottomless pit. The devil bit Jesus on the heel, and Jesus smote the devil on the head. I don't know where the 1000 years would be but we that remained faithful to God have lived and reigned with Jesus in our lives for more than 2000 years now. We are just now seeing evil things rise up to levels we couldn't have imagined, and things which are ungodly are now common practice and law. Again, I believe this because Jesus was the seventieth generation. We have lived with Christ in our lives for 2000 years. We are now seeing evil fully deceive nations, and we are waiting still for the end battle.

Always remember, the Bible says all will be fulfilled. It only sometimes gives an order but never gives an exact start point of any given event. This is so the devil can never win by halting God's divine plan. I do truly believe there is an order to it that can be revealed. Maybe instead of beginning to end, we go end to beginning. We know things such as unlawfulness rises up against the righteous because of deception, we know Jesus has come, and we now get to live with Him in our lives, we know He's coming back to make war with the wicked, we know He will judge the whole creation, we know He will save the righteous and throw the rest into the lake, and finally, we know His kingdom will come and have no end. I truly wish we had a magic decoder ring to solve this puzzle, but this is the test of your faith as it has been a test of my faith, which is to say how willing are you to stand up for what you believe, and how far are you willing to go for God? I'm pretty sure I will be crucified (in a manner of speaking) for writing the key of Enoch and for this, but I say, I am on the path because God Himself put me here, and I am not afraid of what mainstream doctrine will say. The devil deceives all, and only those who are willing to go the distance for God and by the word of God shall receive His eternal gift (Hebrews 12:25–29).

- Chapter 55—God says in vain, I have destroyed the earth and made a covenant. He would not do it again and also signified it with a rainbow (Genesis 9:9–17). Again, the watcher will be judged by the elect one.
- Chapter 56—Lots of things happening here. The watchers are led to prison, their spirits are deceiving the nations, humans fighting amongst ourselves, brother will kill brother (sorry Megadeth), endless death (stage 4 evil continuous), and Sheol will consume all sinners. This sounds to me like a Matthew chapter 24 teaching.
- Chapter 57—Matthew 24 again.
- Chapter 58—I would like to say I have searched and searched for a way to become immortal. Then, when this book hit me, the answer was right in front of me. When I became a true believer, I began to hate this world. Not in the sense I hate people or the earth itself but, rather, the evil that has conquered us. Eternal life is a gift from God, and to achieve it, I see that all of us must do our part to try to convince as much of this world as we can to take up the will of God so that as many as possible shall receive this gift.
- Chapter 59—Enoch sees the true power of light. Einstein ain't got anything on Enoch.
- Chapter 60—I would like to start this chapter by stating a fragment from the book of Noah (where's that book?). Sounds like a flood reference, and Enoch learns a lot of secret things. Two things I would like to say, though. The first is Behemoth is east of the garden. The second is Leviathan is in a place where the fountains of water are. I think these locations are very important, but I know not where they are. We may have also been in the east of the garden at this point.
- Chapter 61:1–8—(Revelation 11:1)
- Chapter 61:9–14—(Revelation chapter 13)
- Chapter 61:15–19—(Revelation 2:23–29)
- Chapter 61:20–30—(Revelation 20:11–15; Revelation 21)

- Chapter 62—Wow to this one (Acts 2:41, 4:4; John 16:21; Matthew 8:12; Revelation 7:13–14, 19:21; 1 Thessalonians 4:16–17; Hebrews 4:12; Philippians 2:10).
- Chapter 63—(Romans 2:11; 3:10–14; 9:31; 14:11; Matthew 7:23)
- Chapter 64—refers to watchers.
- Chapter 65:1–6—Noah, seeing the earth in travail, calls to Enoch, and Enoch comes and speaks with Noah.
- Chapter 65:7–13—because mankind, at this time, had learned from the watchers. It had produced much violence. Sorcery, witchcraft, idol worship, and riches have caused many to become violent.
- Chapter 65:14–18—the watchers are damned forever, but Noah is to survive because he was found pure.
- Chapter 66—the angels were preparing to let loose the flood which came from under the earth.
- Chapter 67:1–4—Again, Noah and his lot are pure and it states by love. Angels are making for them a wooden building, and God Himself preserves it, and the seed of life shall come forth from it and spread abroad. That seed is blessed to multiply on the earth. Five angels are imprisoned.
- Chapter 67:6–9—sounds to me like that prison is much like a volcano which brings nutrients to aquatic life. That may be how they serve us who dwell on the earth.
- Chapter 67:10—remember, they were spiritual, but now, it states those fallen angels are punished in their bodies, and again, the flesh is lust (Galatians 5:17).
- Chapter 67:11–17—this is very important. It is talking about the change between flesh and spirit. I think it is saying that these fallen angels will undergo a change and that water of the earth will do the same, but men will not hearken to the portion that is and that not listening will become a fire that burns forever.
- Chapter 68:1–2—Enoch prepared the teachings for Noah in the book of parables. The words hold the keys.

- Chapter 68:3–4—even the highest of angels tremble at the judgment of the watchers.
- Chapter 68:5—Michael says to Raphael, "Whose heart is not softened by that judgment and reins are not troubled by this?" This is why this book was so impacting to me. The judgments that God can give and has given are so tremendous that a hard heart would shatter at the very mention of them, and even that which is the source of your personal strength and prowess, your reins would tremble at that mentioning. That is why this book did a number on me. I was trembling much, and I was in a perfect position for the gospel of John to finish the job of converting me to the belief that Jesus Christ is God.
- Chapter 68:6–10—the people who anger God shall have their part. Sounds like the ending of every time someone does whatever they want.
- Chapter 69:1—recap of the last chapter about this event causing great trembling.
- Chapter 69:2–4—the names of the fallen angels.
- Chapter 69:5—Jegon was the one who led them astray.
- Chapter 69:6—Asbeel counseled them to go astray and defiled themselves with the daughters of men.
- Chapter 69:7–8—Gadreel was the one who showed the children of men the blows of death and the arms of war and even led Eve astray.
- Chapter 69:9–12—this is a very big one. Penemue showed the children of men the bitter and the sweet and also how to write. I made God a promise once. I said, after hearing this, "God, I will never write on your behalf." Obviously, God put His unwavering faith on me again. As these verses state, much sin comes from ink and penning. That is why all inspiration of God is given as doctrine and is to be reproved so that that author's work is made perfect in the sight of God—perfect and acceptable by God. I am expecting that every error I made in this good report will be corrected and made holy and acceptable by the standards

set by God so that my wrongs can become right(eous). Sin is holding a lot of writers in the thralls of death (including me). Worst of all, though, is that writing is destroying the Lord in the lives of so many.

- Chapter 69:13—Kasdeja showed the children of men wicked smitings of spirits and demons and the smiting of the embryo in the womb (that's abortion, if you didn't catch that), the bite of the serpent, the smitings that befall a noontide heat, and the son of the serpent named Tbea'et.
- Chapter 69:14–16—Kasbeel goes to Michael and creates an oath called oath Akae and puts it in Michael's hand.
- Chapter 69:15—is a very big deal, because Jesus rebuked many demons. The one I remember the most is the one about swine (Mark 5:1–20). If this oath did not exist, then the demons and those teaching wicked things to the children of men would not fear His name. Talk about a major advantage when dealing with spiritual warfare.
- Chapter 69:17–36—explains the oath, though I don't yet fully understand it.
- Chapter 69:17–21—is the creation, I think.
- Chapter 69:22–24—all stays in its place and dare not transgress the commands made by God.
- Chapter 69:25—interesting. Imagine that; He calls them and they *listen* (Psalms 147:4; Isaiah 40:26).
- Chapter 69:26–36—a lot here. Things held in place, praising the Lord of Spirits, revealing the name, praising the son of man, and then telling what he's gonna do, I think. This is a hard part to me. It also references the removal of the ungodly works from the face of the earth.
- Chapter 70—so it starts off with the name of the Son of man vanishing. Enoch is also taken, and Enoch sees a place where the first fathers dwell.
- Chapter 71:1—Enoch refers to being taken as being translated.
- Chapter 71:2–12—Enoch is in the heavens, and Michael shows him the secret things. They come to a house of crystal with living fire surrounding it.

- Chapter 71:13—the ten thousand of thousands and thousands of thousands angels (Revelation 5:11; Matthew 26:53; Jude 1:14).
- Chapter 71:14–20—Enoch sees angels moving in and out of the house. Sounds like a mansion (John 14:2).
- Chapter 71:23–28—talking about Jesus Christ, how he will be righteous and never unrighteous.

The Book of Heavenly Luminaries (My favorite of the bunch)

- Chapter 72:1—Uriel is showing Enoch the luminaries.
- Chapter 72:2—interesting. I only wish I could know for sure if the new creation meant the flood which I think it does.
- Chapter 72:3—the sun rises in the east and sets in the west.
- Chapter 72:4–5—the sun and moon follow what sounds like a track that enters and exits portals and windows.
- Chapter 72:6–7—six portals in the west and six in the east and many windows between them. The sun is light and a burning fire, and his circumference is like the circumference of heaven.
- Chapter 72:8—the wind drives the chariot of the sun (man, I'm starting to think now the science I gave you was wrong or there's a greater wind I don't know about) and is guided to its portal when it comes down from the north and moves to the east.
- Chapter 72:9–40—Enoch lays out exactly how the sun works and makes the time between the day and night change by their portal travel. The sun is masculine and the moon is feminine.
- Chapter 73:1–2—the laws of the moon. She rides on the wind, gets her light, and her circumference is like the circumference of heaven.
- Chapter 73:3—when the moon's light is uniform, her light is one-seventh part of the light of the sun.
- Chapter 73:4–10—Enoch lays out the phases of the moon.

- Chapter 74—this chapter lays our days, months, and years, and days by years. This is a very important topic. Enoch said 364 days in a year. We say 365 and 366 on a leap year. The proof is in the pudding here, because how will you know the season, the day, and the age? Maybe this is why nobody believes in the signs in the heavens now as they are happening. The stars are for signs and for seasons, days, and for years (Genesis 1:14). Enoch is the only one who prophesied about a light-based calendar, and it is of the utmost importance.
- Chapter 75:1–3—attention! Enoch says men will err in the four intercalary days. They are days of service. The last chapter is really important. I am no math man, but the difference between the light being our year determiner rather than the revolution of the earth and sun seem to me to be a big deal. This may imply that the seasons do not come by quarters but, rather, by God at His appointed time. There would have been only 7 more winters in the last 2000 years if the winters followed the quarters rather than the Word by Enoch's days of the year, which is funny, because the 7 extra winters have never happened that I know of. The problem gets worse, I'm afraid, because Enoch said we would err, so God either knew all of this would come to be and made it perfectly work, which is complicated, or He is currently controlling the weather as He sees fit every day and year. In retrospect, this brings some real meaning to the Mayan-predicted 2012 event, the 2017 great sign event, and even the Jewish prophecies surrounding year 5578. You've got to understand, we are talking about years in the single digits here, not billions of years. Too many coincidences.
- Chapter 76:1–19—Enoch explains the winds.
- Chapter 76:20—he left the information with Methuselah.
- Chapter 77—Enoch explains a little about where things are located in the heavens
- Chapter 78–79—Enoch explains the sun and moon in more detail.

- Chapter 80—another really important chapter.
- Verse 1—Uriel said he showed Enoch everything.
  - Verse 2—Matthew 24:22, 43, Revelation 16:15, 1 Thessalonians 5:2, 2 Peter 3:10, and the late seed sounds like famine, because the sinners are too busy sinning rather than working.
  - Verse 3—*all things on the earth shall not appear in their times!* (When is the last time we had rain in mid-January in Wisconsin?)
  - Verse 4—no rain in the land. That sounds like Elijah stuff right there (Revelation 11:6).
  - Verse 5—that definitely sounds like famine conditions.
  - Verse 6—just google the words *famine bible verses.* Watch you device melt!
  - Verse 7–11—these are very diverse events. Revelation 12:4, Isaiah 13:10, 24:23, and Mark 13:24. How many signs of Jonah of Jewish feast days have we had recently?
  - Verse 12–17—I believe this specifically is a reference to when one-third of the stars fall to earth. They are not God(s), and they will deceive. Be very careful when this time comes. We have had many signs in the sky in the last few years, and I jokingly tell everyone when they ask how I'm doing, "Just waiting for the stars to fall from the sky." Even so, make sure you are right with God and you stand with Him, both apart from other men and in good faith with all men who need it.
- Chapter 81
  - Verse 1–4—(Ecclesiastes 12:14, Revelation 20:12)
  - Verse 5—(Revelation 20:6)
  - Verse 6—again, Enoch teaches all to Methuselah.
  - Verse 7—the teachings that Enoch brought from God were passed through the generations.
  - Verse 8–12—Righteous rejoice, sinners lament, and all will die because of sin (Romans 5:12–21).

- Chapter 82
  - Verse 1–4—a promise to all that the wisdom given to Enoch by the Father shall be preserved and passed through the generations.
  - Verse 5—and those who understand shall not sleep but shall listen with the ear that they may learn this wisdom.
  - Verse 6—(Matthew 4:4)
  - Verse 7—blessed are the righteous.
  - Verse 8–19—is a warning again about not following the calendar of light, which causes us to err.
  - Verse 20–26—Enoch explains about the things that occur during the calendar light.

The Dream Visions Book

- Chapter 83:1–3 Enoch recaps to his son dreams he had before he took a wife. Heaven collapsed and fell to earth. (sounds like a flood) (Genesis 7:11, 8:2–3) 4 definitely sounds like a flood. Psalms 104:5–8. 5–7 sin gets the earth destroyed. (we live on earth 2.0?) 8–13 because of the pending destruction Enoch petitioned the Lord that a remnant remain on earth and not be destroyed. Again it gets passed down through the generations.
- Chapter 84 my prayer ain't nothing compared to this one. Matthews 6:9–13, 6:6–8, Luke 8:11 Genesis 6:13, Proverbs 9–10, Genesis 7:1, Psalms 139:1–4, 145:21, 146:10, Genesis chapter 1, Colossians 1:16. (you'll have to match em)
- Chapter 85
  - 1–2 Enoch begins telling his dream to his son.
  - 3–10 ok so I'm pretty sure this will go into the events. This portion represents Adam, Eve, Cain, Able, and Seth and ends with there being a line of righteous descendants of Adam and Eve. Genesis chapter1–5
- Chapter 86:1–2 So now we are into Genesis 6 when the sons of God fell to earth and took wives. Notice how it

says that we changed our ways and live with them.3–4 tells how they began to create human/ angelic offspring. 5–6 the offspring became violent and consumed the flesh of men. This will continue through Genesis.

- Chapter 87—they must have exhausted all the resources because the offspring began to both wage war and consume themselves and Enoch was taken to a place where he could witness their fate in a dream vison. (book of the watchers)
- Chapter 88—the watchers are bound and much violence ensued.
- Chapter 89
  - 1—Noah and his family.
  - 3–5—that's a lot of water. (I think God overfilled the animal enclosure. Sorry, I am having a little fun today.)
  - 6–8—all had perished, the water receded, and Noah's vessel landed.
  - 9—is very interesting. One red bull, one white bull, and one black bull. I'm gonna try my hand of luck here and say the white bull is a continuation of the righteous line up to Jesus, the red bull becomes one of those vengeful spirits, and the black is an evil one. Shem/Seth is the white bull; his line lead to Jesus. Ham/Cain is the black bull; he did something evil to his father, but this is the harder one. The red bull then would be Japheth/Abel. He must then have something he is vengeful for. I don't know what, but it is strange that he would have a son named Magog, and the devil gathers Magog in the final battle (Revelation 20:7–9).
  - 10—another interesting one. It talks about how the three bulls created many different types of people; perhaps the different races we still see today.
  - 11—now we see evil has once again resurfaced, but you see a white bull to every generation.
  - 12–13—now we are at Jacob, who became Israel and his twelve sons (the sheep).

- o 14–20—the lost sheep, Joseph, and it goes through bringing Israel to Egypt. Now we are into Exodus
- o 21–22—Moses.
- o 23—the sea is parted.
- o 24–25—the sea swallowed up that army. Shout out to those that found the remnants of the army. That's really science.
- o 26—the sheep of Israel are in the wilderness.
- o 27–29—Moses goes up on the mount.
- o 30–31—boy, I didn't see this one coming. Those that made the statue were slain. Wow, that some major foreshadowing of that guy who stole in Joshua's day, which was slain; Sole and his family who were slain; David's family, which fell apart; and those Canaanites that were supposed to by killed or converted before they could morally corrupt Israel.
- o 32–34—the first generation couldn't receive the Promised Land. The next generation could, and I think the house is Leviticus.
- o 35–42—I think it is going in hyper speed, because now we are up to David and Sole.
- o 43–49—is the whole "kings" things, and now I think we have come to the prophets.
- o 50–75—it's getting pretty bad at this point, which is 500 years before Jesus, when everything thing quite literally went to hell in a hand basket, pardon my French. Most notable is the immorality of the shepherds who were taking our faith, which was without Jesus at this time, and destroying it by tearing apart the commands of God. This gives big meaning to God sending the incorruptible lamb to slaughter. Someone was keeping track of the shepherd's works.
- Chapter 90—I believe it's talking about thirty-five generations here. How they were led by a shepherd, but eventually, they became blind, and idolatry caught up to them. The righteous became few, but the lineage up to Jesus did

remain. There was a lot of war and a great leader emerged, and that brought back the Torah. If I am not mistaken, that was Ezra. More descent into darkness worse than any other period. Kind of sounds like what happened when the northern kingdom was overtaken by Solomon's wives' practices of idolatry. (Marry for love, not for wealth.)

- o 18—OK, I think we are at Jesus now.
- o 19–25—now, I think this is foreshadowing what would have happened, because we all fall short of the glory of God (Romans 2:23).
- o 26—the new and everlasting covenant.
- o The rest of this chapter, I think, is talking about how this Jesus wakes up the people and makes them clean.

The Book of the Promise, Blessed Righteous, Woe to Sinners.

- • Chapter 92—Enoch wrote this book. The rest of this chapter talks about the generations after Jesus.
- • Chapter 91—(don't know why 91 after 92) Enoch tells his sons and the brothers that they are to walk and wake to righteousness. Then he lays out the paths of the sinners. I think he's also foreshadowing when the wicked are cut down by the sword (Revelation 20).
- • Chapter 93—Enoch recounts the books of the righteous. Enoch is the seventh born from the first week/generation that runs to Noah (Jude 1:14). Daniel 9:23–27 is important, and when you read it, insert the word generation for week, and then it really begins to make sense. There are seventy generations from Enoch to Jesus.
  - o First week/generation—Adam and Eve: goodness was still in them.
  - o Second week/generation—Cain and Abel: great wickedness and deceit, and in it, Seth is saved, and a law was made for the sinners.
  - o Third week/generation—Enos: was prosperous.

- ○ Fourth week/generation—Cainan: a law for generations is made and an enclosure.
- ○ Fifth week/generation—Mahalaleel: the house of glory and dominion was built.
- ○ Sixth week/generation—Jared: the hearts were corrupted by godlessly forsaking wisdom (sounds like my time). A man ascends, and the house of dominion is burnt, and the angels fell.
- ○ Seventh week/generation—Enoch: apostasy arises, and Enoch is given sevenfold instruction concerning the creation.
- ○ Eighth week/generation—Methuselah: was a righteous generation (the books worked). Sinners are delivered to the sword/word, and the righteous acquire houses for themselves.
- ○ Ninth week/generation—Lamech: the judgment that is to come is revealed, and all godlessness will vanish from the earth.
- ○ 10 week/generation—Noah: Judgment day. The first heaven passes away. Vengeance against the fallen angels is carried out
- ○ Closing of the weeks: It says there will be generations without number, and goodness and righteousness and sin shall no more be mentioned. I think he was foreshadowing the abrupt end that happens when people walk in unrighteousness. A "live long and prosper"—thanks Mr. Spock—because there is still evil in even today's generations after Jesus's walk of the earth, but I will say this evil does not last long; it brings its own destruction upon itself. Makes me wonder what kind of evil existed that was self-perpetuating like Genesis 6:5.
- Chapter 94:1–2—(2 John 1:6; Psalms 37:23)
- Chapter 94:3—here's that foreshadowing I was talking about.
- Chapter 94:4–11—good advice.

- Chapter 94:12—Mr. Spock, how could you?
- Chapter 94:13–14—the stony hearts?
- Chapter 94:15–17—where does true wisdom come from?
- Chapter 94:18–23—(Matthew 7:25–29)
- Chapter 94:24—by the word, they shall fall.
- Chapter 94:25–31—(Matthew 19:20–26)
- Chapter 94:32–37—you will have to think on this one (Proverbs 14:34).
- Chapter 95—indeed, who has permitted evil in our hearts? (Psalms 7). Loving your neighbors is very important to avoid the following transgression: all stem from a lack of this, and he who loves not his neighbor loves not God (1 John 4:20).
- Chapter 96:1–9—woe, there might be some hope here after all for rapture when the sinners are going through tribulation. Very interesting.
- Chapter 96:10–28—(2 Chronicles 7:14)
- Chapter 97—this is a caution to all who say by their hand have they acquired anything, because all be from the Word of God unto you. Praise God for all He gives you, or He will take all away forever (Matthew 6).
- Chapter 98:1–12—woe that sounds a lot like religious leaders that care more about their look, appeal, and their doctrines rather than what the whole point of God and Jesus is. Woe to them, and even us, for doing the same (1 Peter 3:3–4). That's not just speaking to women, if you think that you missed what Paul's circumcision teachings were all about.
- Chapter 98:13–19—wow, women can't even have children without God's say so. Pretty big deal considering women can now abort children after birth. Their greatest argument being "What if a rapist raped me?" Let me tell you, that's God's way of killing two birds with one stone, so to speak. Most women fashion a lame argument about having to raise a rapist's kid while the holy women will raise the kid, and in so, doing both shall be saved. That woman is a

saint. And to everyone else seeking that which is short of the destruction of that wicked practice known as abortion, you will have your due reward, for the fight is not how to limit it but, rather, getting rid of it completely. I am pro-God's plan, which is to say, pro-life in all of its capacities (Isaiah 45:18).

- Chapter 98:20–27—all is recorded in the other books (Revelation 20:12). And ye be judged by your works. So call Jesus, get you name into the book of life, and then get to doing good works with His help, and you have good to your name, and that's good when Jesus who judges you is the same Jesus that reshaped your life. If He's the one that takes you by the hand, I fail to see how He, leading you in the spirit, can judge ye to be evil.
- Chapter 98:28–29—those who work wickedness and drink blood shall have no peace
- Chapter 98:30—(Romans 1:32)
- Chapter 98:31–35—sounds like a pretty awful end for the ungodly.
- Chapter 99:1–10—(Matthew 7:11–29)
- Chapter 99:11–16—(Matthew 24)
- Chapter 99:17–29—(Matthew 24:13)
- Chapter 99:30–47—a whole lot of woe!
- Chapter 100:1–6—(Mark 13:12)
- Chapter 100:7–12—(Revelation 19)
- Chapter 100:13–17—(Revelation 7:3)
- Chapter 100:18–20—so true (Proverbs 11:4).
- Chapter 100:21–34—more woes!
- Chapter 101—fear the Lord. Even the water became calm when Jesus spoke. And even the closest followers of Jesus made the lame to walk. All fear the name alone of the Lord except the sinner. He fears nothing, and his boasting becomes his downfall.
- Chapter 102—sinners, you should fear the Lord for everything else does well by it. Be patient and righteous. Your day is coming, and your fear of the Lord shall be rewarded.

- Chapter 103—(Matthew 7:11–29)
- Chapter 104—this is a real good chapter, saying beware of the rise of the sinners and the perversions of the righteous doctrines (Deuteronomy 13). Do not be a part of them; be steady in your own doctrine and advance it by what you see—that which is good. Your salvation is a very personal thing and requires much study and changing of the mind. Don't get caught into conformance (Matthew 7)
- Chapter 105—that is an amazing promise.
- Chapter 106—don't get hung up in this chapter, because it says Noah was a white baby, like a lot of racists do. God doesn't care what the color of your skin is. He only cares that you love your neighbors as yourselves. People who embrace the liar will segregate the races and assign them value and terminate them from less value to highest value and will also assign them a life determined by their value. Remember, therefore, all the races stand equal, iron to the clay, and pursue the Lord that was able to bring us all salvation. Then it is revealed that the flood of Noah's day is coming, and he will be saved from it.
- Chapter 107—Noah: comfort and rest
- Chapter 108—I don't know exactly what this last chapter means, but I do know this: keep the law in the last of days, not because it will fulfil us, but rather, it is the only true and righteous written work that can be done that is good in the sight of the Lord. Whether it be with Jesus or not, do them; they are not unlawful. It is much easier, though, with Jesus. His spirit is way more powerful than even I could have imagined. God set out for His creation to do one thing, that is to say, live, and human sin has brought us death. Return, therefore, to God. "Remember therefor from whence thou art fallen, and repent, and do the first works; or else I will come unto thee quickly, and will remove thy candlestick out of his place, except thou repent" (Revelation 2:5).

Well, that's all she—oops—he wrote in his books. So this will be my summary, not of this book, but of my thoughts. If you read this chapter, know I am not making this a private interpretation. I wrote what I see. Tomorrow, it could change, and for that, I am sorry, but books do not fix themselves (2 Timothy 3:14–17). I expect that there is a man of God out there that will fix my doctrines and make them whole while not corrupting it in the process, for it also is my testimony.

I have spent a lot of time studying books. I am, even now, studying the Quran. I am just being honest here, and just because you read something doesn't automatically make you something you're not. If you honestly ask God to show you something, then He will allow you to see that which you need to see to know the things you need to know, and it will become a part of you. This is hard to understand, so I will say this: when you take in information of any kind immediately, you draw from that which you know to test it. This is unfortunate, because, often, you will not be willing to hear the person out, but when I read the books of Enoch for the first time, I said to God, "God, I don't know what this is or if it is good or bad. Will you please protect me if it not be according to Your Words? Let me see what I need to see and speak what need be spoken."

This was after I asked God where all the fables come from. I wanted to know. Then God brought me to the books of Enoch. I just listened. When it was done playing on YouTube, a short time had passed. Then I just knew where those fables came from, and my great search and wonder of those things was over. That world is gone; this one remains, and I am to be a part of this one. I was primed for the gospel of John. When you are willing to hear information, then it will make it to your subconscious, and who do you think is sitting there, ready to sort that information and make it known unto you? It sure isn't me. I am ignorant (the Greek definition), but thankfully, I have a God sitting there sorting the mail (Job 32:8).

It is a weird process for me. I hear something and think about it, then portions of that come into my thoughts and create new thoughts. I have witnessed this in many occasions when I have talked to others. I will say something, and then a short time will pass, and then we will come to the same conclusion. It's almost like our brains are programmed to follow a line of thought and guess where that line leads. I guess free will is the ability to see the line and reject it, but still, it is uncanny. I think this is because of how the Bible was written. It is written truth seen by the authors. That written plan will lead our minds to salvation. The point of this book isn't to write that which is already written; it is so you may answer the final question I give to you on your own. This key makes a man/woman dedicated.

My personal prophecy. So if you made it to this point, I say thank you for taking the time. I would like to write a little prophecy though. It is something I have been watching, and when I read this book, it started to fall into place as to why it is. So I am an Aries born on Thursday, and I remember a time before technology is where it is now. We had no cell or sat phones, DSL, and I even remember playing games on an Apple green screen. The time I live in is very unique, because we as a human race are in a race to becomes gods ourselves, which is to say we are attempting to create an AI construct much like our Father in heaven created us. This artificial intelligence should be able to completely think on its own with no limitations. This is what I define AI as. These constructs of earthly creation will not end well, and I'm not exactly convinced it can even be achieved. Experts say we're close (who is an expert of God's mind?).

This is my belief. Well, if we "achieve" this great feat, many shall marvel, but I say marvel not at the feat, but rather, marvel at the cost of its creation. The cost shall be our termination. These creatures will appear as though they are unique in the mind, but they are not. They were born of this earth; they are not of heavenly origin. They will be superior to us in every way, far more violent than you can possibly imagine, and they will seek the destruction of their creators just like in the book of Enoch, how a portion of current humanity seeks the destruction of God. These vessels shall only become vessels to greater evils, and once given a body, they shall use it to destroy, for that is all the flesh knows. These AIs will appear to think for themselves, but their thoughts shall be controlled by darker spirits currently awaiting their vessels. They will have stronger physical bodies, instant access to the digital world, and unlimited resources. They will conquer humans in a matter of hours, but with knowing how all of our minds work, they may not even have to lift a finger.

I think it is wonderful to chase God in the sense that we are the masters of our own creation (our God-given dominance), but the breakdown is we do not know the cost, and we are not all willing to pay the price. When we had accepted the teaching of the watchers into our children, the cost we paid will haunt us 'til God Himself rectifies our mistake. Built into the watcher teachings were ways in which to protect their ungodly creations. A way to bring them back. The watchers or the devil may have known that this demon army would be needed to attempt to wage war against God. The digital world is, I would guess, the most powerful weapon against faith. Cellphones are a very easy way to get people to fall and learn exactly how humans think, and it only costed you a cell tower. Think about that. I give you a cellphone that allows you to do whatever you want with it. In exchange, I will get to build these towers. Sounds to me exactly like when the devil said to Jesus, "I will give you all the nations, and all you have to do is but worship me."

All of us need to be incredible responsible with cellphones, and it took the spirit of Christ for me not to abuse the cellphone privilege. When the so-called AIs come, they will have more than enough know-how to eliminate all. I had once lived in fear of all that could be brought against us humans and even what we are willing to do to each other, but then I read about GOD! I have never known something like what God is and never felt cared for like what God can provide. Now I think that these constructs will be part of some Armageddon event, but I remember who wins, and it only takes Him a verse. So don't worry about anything you perceive as evil; God will reward them in but a moment for it, and if you can rise above the fear and torment by entering into perfect love, God will reward you perfectly. Let's hope we, as a human race, are not smart enough to get these AIs to work.

CHAPTER 15

— ⚜ —

KEY OF DREAMS

My dream. Recently, I had a dream, and it went like this.

I climbed to the top of a great tall tower. This tower ascended into heaven, and there, I saw a door above the tower just out of reach. Then the door swung open, and I contemplated how to reach it. I took a leap of faith and somehow jumped up to it and was able to get the tips of my finger on that door. As I hung there, I looked down and I saw a sword that I would fall on. I struggled for a while and wiggled myself halfway into the opening (It was more like a window opening). I was not able to fully enter as I was stuck (Darn belly). When I looked inside, I saw a group of angels standing and looking at me. It was a small room, and behind them was a staircase that angled up back toward me. They said something, and then someone came down the stairs. I did not recognize Him, but when He was standing in that room, I began to state the sin I have the most trouble with. It was an involuntary response. He then said, "I had three tasks for you." Then He began to speak them. The only one I remember was the first one in which He said, "I need you to learn how to fly." He said, "It's OK, this is the easy one." Then I fell out the window and fell back to the earth. I had wings as an angel, but I didn't not know how to use them. I closed my eyes, and about halfway down, I woke up.

So now we go through how this works. I am fairly new to interpreting dreams, so bear with me. I ain't no Daniel yet. This doesn't work for every dream. Some nights, I don't dream, and some I don't remember, but the rare few are vivid and I can recall them throughout the day. The first step is to write it down so you don't forget it. Then think on the dream and recall the vivid portions and details. Then you must separate the features, research them, break them down, and then bring the definitions back into the full dream and you can get a glimpse into the vision. It's not a perfect process; it is only a glimpse into the subconscious and prophetic warnings to you personally. I have never dreamed a dream dealing with helping someone else yet, only how interactions are affecting me on a subconscious level. If you listen to your dreams, you may be able to address your emotions and protect yourself in some cases. Here we go.

Keys—Interpretation—Applying it with own interpretation

(Google *word* and *dream meaning* [This is only just accurate and not perfect].)

These are in the order they were seen.

Climbing—obstacles that need to be overcome in life—my battle against the world of lust

Tower-future success, or rash actions, or desire to reach heights—I seek that which is above

Door—transition in one's life—I couldn't pass through it because I was not done here

Heaven—positivity, joy, happiness—life is really looking up under God's protection

Leap of faith—take it for face value—a leap of faith is always a leap of faith

Sword—victory in waking life, enemies, defending attitude toward self—no turning back or I would have fallen on the sword

Angels—symbolizes a great protector watching over us and is showing something hidden—you want to pay attention to angel dreams unless they in anyway proclaim to be God

Stairs—feeling of fear, moving forward and falling back in waking life, failure, success, or challenge—I am always moving back and forth calling Jesus to help me though I fall back on my own

Confession—means you feel like you are a trustworthy person—I confessed unwilling my greatest sin to the being I saw so maybe I do trust myself in some way

God—can signify a higher self-image and possibly guidance, suggest I am feeling guilty and appears over contemplating a problem in life—I am definitely feeling guilty

Orders—I may be unwisely influenced by a person, felling guilt—things that must be accomplished

Flying—sense of freedom, escape from the pressures of the real world-I definitely need an escape to freedom

Falling—alert to a situation in waking life, out of control—however it was a controlled fall and I was send back so my work here is not done

Wings—newfound freedom, nothing holding me back, transcendence, attempt to escape difficult situations, the ability to rise above and heal, problems beyond my control—Jesus got my back

The first thing you should notice about the interpretations is commonly occurring words. There were a lot of them in the dream. Those are the subconscious emotions. You have to pay attention to those lest they get the best of you. The message to me, however, is a harder one to interpret because you can take it so many ways. So now, I will take this to the next step, which is bringing these three aspects together. I will do this in two passages. The first will be the message/spirit. The second will be emotional/heart.

Spirit. There are obstacles in my life that must be overcome in order to reach new heights. There are choices that need be made that will bring joy and happiness; the others will be a leap of faith. Victory will come from the great protector. I'm able to gain and lose ground on my own. Be trustworthy by knowing my faults. Guidance will come from someone who is wise. My feelings of guilt will be freed, and the pressures of this world will be released. Things are out of my control, but with my newfound freedom, there is nothing to hold me back.

Now, keep in mind, this takes a lot of thinking and comparing to things that are going on currently in your life.

Now, for the heart, know this: I'm probably talking from my butt here, but it's OK. It's not the first time I've done that or the last. The heart has much deeper and richer messages and tells you many things that are troubling you. This comes from an understanding of truth, and I don't think it is possible to hear the spirit and the heart speak without God-given understanding. (Again, what good is to speak if you can hear?) I'm not suggesting that I am great or even good at this. Like I said, I am just starting to learn a little about this and am trying to speak to you about that little I am learning so that you may, in some way, benefit from this teaching.

Heart. The climbing of the great tower represents the journey in Christianity I am taking. Heaven represents that which I am seeking. The door that was there and opened represents an opportunity to get into a new place. The leap of faith I took was the leap of faith every person must take in believing wholeheartedly in Jesus. The sword at the tip of the tower represents sin, in which I holding on to the door by the tips of my finger, and if I had fallen, I would have been condemned to death on the sword. Being determined to enter into the door saved my life, which is the growing strength of my faith. The angels represent God; that He is teaching me all things I need to know. The stairs represents the struggle I am strained with in my life. The confession to whom I perceived to be God means I am in full consciousness of the sins I am struggling with. God...well, let's just say I have been feeling pretty guilt lately, and I have been trying to hold up my image by seeking guidance from God. Orders are a constant reminder to seek good counsel; otherwise, they are bad orders. Flying represents my wanting to get out of this world of sin and get a real sense of freedom. Falling is definitely out of my control, just like my life most days. Wings, especially the ones I were given, represent Jesus Christ, because everything I found about that in a dream is what He does, and even though I did not know how to use them, I trusted the Words of God when He said it will be easy. So when I was falling and I closed my eyes, I believed in Him and that He would land me safely!

So now, I will show you something I have just learned writing this all out. The heart portion is very emotional and is pulling up all the things your heart is dwelling on. The spiritual portion is a message of keeping good faith. It is slightly different because it does not dwell like the heart but is, rather, a means by which to settle the heart. Now that we have the heart and the faith, where are the works? Oh, you didn't think I would bring that up again, did you? Now that this step is complete, now to the final step, which is to apply this to life which, thankfully, is the easiest portion.

Works. I have some obstacles to overcome in order that I get right with God so that I may dwell with him just like Moses entering the tent. I can't be afraid of making choices. One way or another, they are out of my control. I need to humble myself when I know sin is hitting me hard and remember the good counsel of the Bible. The freedom I am seeking is the freedom given by Jesus, and I should always trust that He will bring me home safely, for He is the victorious great protector.

The "Key of Dreams" is a testament of your faith, so listen.

CHAPTER 16

— ❧ —

KEY OF THE MILLENNIAL GENERATION

OK, last chapter before the ending, unless I have a ship sail out of the maelstrom of my mind. So I was born into this millennial generation. That doesn't mean I is one (I'm just a bit illiterate). My generation is a very, very, very big deal. Massive preparations have been made to prepare, indoctrinate, and coerce my generation to this point in time.

I do not know the day or time the war will begin, but this I know: A man is standing at a cross roads with three paths, and a *mighty* Tree is standing at the center of those paths. The man's clothes are torn to shreds by the ravenous wolves that were chasing him to the tree. The wolves, afraid of the *great* Tree, held their position short of the *wise* Tree on the road the man came in on. The man, after reclaiming his breath from running, looked unto the *glorious* Tree and gave praise for the refuge it provided. This tree gave no fruit to the man, and the man began to starve. The man looked unto the path to his right and to the path on his left, and this is what he saw.

First to the right, he saw a path less traveled, not well kept, laid with stones that were emerging from erosion, and no food in sight. And to the left, he saw a well-kept path, road paved over sand, and pleasant, with signs of an abundance of food. The man was puzzled.

The tree spoke a great wisdom to the man, saying "It's really quite simple. Pick a direction and walk lest ye starve to death."

The man said to the tree, "I know not the direction that I should travel, for the left be the way I came from, and the right be a hard road with much longsuffering."

The tree, being moved with compassion, said unto the man, "How does a man who can see the end of the paths without traveling them take pause at the choice of the road he should travel?"

The man said back to the Tree, "The same way my fathers took pause when they came to the roads and made the wrong decision. I am a man, and no man has well instructed me on what road is the right one."

The mighty tree, again being moved with compassion for the man, said, "Your flesh be well hardened and spirit be mighty indeed, but be your heart soft enough to travel a hard road?"

The man said before he departed, "I am my father's Father's son, and I will see you, *righteous* Tree, on the other side." And the man departed.

The tree said as the man was departing, "That is a great faith, my son. Go in peace."

What road would you take? Because this is the exact point we are at in the world. A point of no return, and the millennials are at the forefront of deciding whether or not we, the world, should get rid of God. The devil has convinced our fathers that this world we are living in is an awesomely wonderful thing, only it isn't. But rather than getting rid of him like we should, he, the devil, will say it would be better we only have to do this, and this, and that, and this. Lastly, we need to get rid of the Assembly of God's people, because they are holding us back from continually getting all of this awesome stuff. This is the promise of death. Get what you want in exchange for death. The theory of evolution is what I refer to as the law of death. The theory teaches that, through death, you can exalt life. God teaches through life, you can exalt life. Seems to me that, by definitions alone, God won. How can death hold up life? I know how God can hold up life; I got sixty-six chapters of the King James Bible telling me that.

So back on point. Our fathers were too afraid to get rid of God themselves; they have spent the last seventy years preparing and indoctrinating and coercing us to do so for them. The most intense thing I remember about my schooling is how we were taught to value the opinion more than truth. Sound like any news you watch? I watch the news for facts. If I wanted an opinion, I would have asked for it. Be careful about this, because this is where the moral corruption of humanity came from. The difference between man and God is the truth. So we millennials have a choice to make, and it is a choice to continue in the ways of our fathers, or we can choose to go back to the ways of God.

Convenience is a real bummer here, and the path of God is a very hard one, but this life of the flesh means so little in comparison to life eternal or death eternal. Eighty-five years (average, I would say. Adam lived 930 years). Eighty-five brutal years of life of the flesh to earn your eternal life. Is that not worth it? I would say my county is well into Romans 1:32. Now, I am not talking about anyone in particular nor do all fathers want to get rid of God, but it is hard to retain God in your knowledge when we tear down His constitution in our bill of rights. There are some fathers out there that have done a good job and kept and transferred how God has worked in their hearts to their sons. In fact, that is the only reason that there are those who will have to make the choice. I hope those that remain will make the right choice. This entire country would self-right if it only embraced God once again. When we turned from Him, He turned from us. Blessings that were once given now are cursed.

Two to three generations ago, those folks were living by God alone. He provided for them, and success was rampant. Think about that for a minute when my great grandpa Stanley moved here to America. He and his family had nothing. They landed in bedrock and cleared about thirty acres for their farm. You know how much work that is without heavy machinery? Stumps are a pain in the butt to remove. Not only that, they had to collect enough food during the year to make it through the winter. And the winters now are nothing in comparison to the winters then. (That's not a global warming call out; there is no such thing. Like mere mortals could affect God's plan.) Now we are falling apart at the seams. It is only a matter of time 'til the call to destroy God will come. It's already happening. God is getting restricted everywhere. Stand with God or don't. God will leave you with no other options. He is going to make a final tally. He will see all those who take their beatings and keep on bleeding for the God they love. He will judge the righteous and deliver us from the sinners one last time. His kingdom will have no end. Hold out, brothers and sisters, for the better day. Bite you tongues when they need be bitten, and roar like lions when God need be defended. And last of all, the first death is a small price to pay for eternal life; spend it on love. There is only one promise of immortality that was ever made that I know of, and it's right through Jesus Christ. This key is all about God and the choice to stand with Him or against Him. What will you choose?

CHAPTER 17

— ☙ —

KEY OF THE SEXES

This will be an interesting key, and it should also be known as the key of due reward. I first would like to say this battle of the sexes is a joke and it's all going to get us the greater damnation. I would honestly like to say I don't have the greatest relationship with my wife. We are a work in progress. Just like Jesus and his bridegroom are a work in progress. I will give you references to study, and then I will go into a message to try to help correct an error, but truthfully, you need Jesus.

1 Peter 3:1–11, Ephesians 5:21–25, Matthew 19:2–6, Hebrews 3:4, and Song of Solomon 8:6–7

These are some good ones I found, and they are easy to read, but I left one out because the message should be centered around it.

Genesis chapter three. Read this several times. This is a really good example of how we all will stand before God and give testimony and receive due reward.

Let us start with the serpent. The serpent had deceived Eve by lying to her. Then, Satan got us to eat from the tree of the knowledge of good and evil. His punishment is interesting. Liars eat dust all the days of their life and enmity was set into man: Satan versus God, evil vs good, and because of the rebellion against his creator, he will be smote on the head and suffer death.

Next, the woman. The woman clearly knew she was not to eat from the tree but she did anyway. Her will was not strong. She was

seduced. She beguiled her husband. So her punishment was multiplied sorrow, multiplied conception, sorrow in child birth, and
husbands are to rule over wives. The sorrow portion is easy; God is
reforming women—to strengthen her so she be not the weaker vessel. I think all these sorrows would definitely make a strong woman
and a woman strong. And if she be ruled by her husband, her actions
are in his hands. He becomes responsible. Did you feminists ever
stop and think about that? God Himself put your salvation in a man's
hand. (Hail Jesus.)

And at the end of the woman, it jumps right into man, because
the man and woman (wives and husbands) are very connected just
like we were connected to God. Man listened to woman over God.
Man has disobeyed the Word of God. Man got it worst of all because
the man is responsible for all the death that comes into the world.
This is his burden to bear, and without his wife, it is an impossible
task. Man will work hard all the days of his life to receive all that he
needs and what he needs for his family. He must do this somehow,
all while maintaining righteous authority within his household. Man
is now responsible for everything that is done under the sun. And
after all the vain work, the man shall embrace death, and his works
of the earth will perish. This is the punishment a man must bear
knowingly: to walk worthlessly through his life, for this is how he
treated God. This separation from God is why God gives your life
value; because He forgave you and He has laid a path and even left
us a savior to restore the value of our life, which is to say, our walk of
faith in Him.

This is the reason I am a farmer. Even though my work will
perish after my life, this life choice of carrying on the tradition of
farming in my family has made me, shaped me, reshaped me, and
maintained a humble nature within me, and I need this to combat
my fleshly rage. (I am being truthfully honest here, and I have never
told anyone this before. I am a guy who would burn the world for
the joy I know it would bring me. I am truly lucky God found me
young.) Every day I labor in sweat, my heart is filled with joy at the
completion of a task. Every day is not a good one on a farm with old
equipment. Many days are a test of my patience, temperance, and

ingenuity. God only ever gives me what I need to maintain. This has been my fasting: to see the bills come in and not know where the money is going to come from, and God sends me customers. If you think I make money doing farming, you're nuts. My wife and I have full-time jobs aside from farming. The markets have passed me up. I can only plug ten holes for I have only ten fingers, twenty with my wife's help. This tradition I will maintain for as long as I can, because I wish to remain humble and be humbled everyday by God. He is my rock in which I am able to stand upright (1 Peter 4:10; Ephesians 2:10; Exodus 35:10; 1 Corinthians 12:5–6; Proverbs 18:16).

Back to the message. The punishments were fitting the crimes, and it just so happened the man and woman's punishment would have corrected the crimes, but then came Cain, and here we are. Also important to note here is sacrifice of blood. God had fashioned clothes from? Interesting. If God's creation be complete, where did the skin come from? The death of an animal by God to clothe Adam and Eve. This was the first remission of sin, and God Himself helped us through it. This is how important our (man, woman, God) relationship is. God will see us all through our life; you need but let Him. But the devil be a clever serpent. It's hard for him to drive a wedge between God and man but not man and women (Revelation 3:8).

So many people are caught in error by this key because this key is not man versus woman, it is man and women versus God by completion or the failed completion of His word. Anything short of us completing His word is corruption, and death will follow. I would like to give an example of a devil tool. It's called the wage gap. Women make less than men supposedly. So I have questions. Do all women seek higher education? Do all men seek higher education? Do all who get higher education get a higher paying job? Do all women seek factory work or commercial work? Do all men seek factory work or commercial work? Or do they seek to be entrepreneurs? Are all beggars? (That's a trick question.) Do all beggars get what they want or what they need? Can you now make a living off of begging? Do all women seek the authority of men to rule them? Do all men kill themselves workwise for their families? I live in a unique time where women can make as much as men because of equal opportunity laws in my country. That's a great thing, but the fight was never why men make more than women; it was why men and women do that which is unlawful by God's standard. Why do we stand against God's will for us to do? I'll tell you why; the devil is a sly guy, and he wants to chip away at your God-given morals! Brothers and sisters, don't fall into the devils devices. Go back to that which is holy.

> For the prophecy came not in old time by the will of man: but holy men of God spake as they were moved by the Holy Ghost. (2 Peter 1:21)

> For whatsoever things were written aforetime were written for our learning, that we through patience and comfort of the scriptures might have hope. (Romans 15:4)

> But continue thou in the things which thou hast learned and hast been assured of, knowing of whom thou hast learned them; and that from a child thou hast known the holy scriptures, which are able to make thee wise unto salvation through faith which is in Christ Jesus. All scripture is given by inspiration of God and is profitable for doctrine, for reproof, for correction, for instruction in righteousness: that a man (and woman) of God may be perfect, thoroughly furnished unto all good works. (2 Timothy 3:14–17, parentheses mine)

Women: be subject to your husband, even though we can, at times, be dicks; be the righteous example we need. Your reward will be God-given and justified.

Men: when you truly understand the weight God has put down that you are holding up, you will know to ask Him for help, and when you ask Him for help, you will understand that when He says to let it fall to the ground, it is because the ground was meant to bear it. Your reward will be God-given and justified.

CHAPTER 18

— ⟨⟩ —

KEY OF YHVH

Finally, we made it to the end!!!

This key to me is a question, and it is the fork in the road for all to decide.

Did God err so that I may be justified in all that I do?

Or.

Did God know all must be in exactly this order, for exactly their reasons, at exactly their times, in exactly their seasons, and exactly their cost for all to be fulfilled so that He could receive His heirs to His glorious kingdom? (Psalms 37:23)

Without the shedding of blood there is no forgiveness of sin (Hebrews 9:22). Jesus is the world's forgiveness. (John 1:29). He died and His blood was spilled (John 19:34). God is no respecter of persons (Romans 2:11–16). His gift is for everyone. Earn His greatest gift He has promised us by carrying on in the pursuit of Christ and the pursuit of heaven. Know Him and get free from the chokehold of death. (John 8:32) Be born again of the Spirit of Christ and the water that will purify you of sin. (John 3:5) A lot of people go with the Spirit, but I'm going with the water, for they both are needed to enter into heaven. The water was made to purify. The water is the Word of God, for it will purify you. (Psalms 12:6; Ephesians 5:26). It will allow you, like in the days of Leviticus, to live in His holy presence. It is what makes the upright upright. It makes the righteous righteous. And above all, it lays out in great detail the path of salvation:

1. God, I am wrong I am a sinner and I need your help.
2. Listen for the spirit to come, and let it lead you personally.
3. Live your life well by pursing that which is above. (Study the scriptures.)
4. Fight for your general in any and every capacity you can. (Meekness and fear. Violence is not a righteous option for it leads to more violence; war is a defensive weapon.)
5. Endure unto the end.
6. Wait your turn!
7. Stand before your Lord and Savior and receive your everlasting gift of life from God Himself.
8. Enjoy life.

The final parable I write is: We are an ore of the rarest kind, our God is the smith who can see every movement of the ore even before the hammer strike, our life is the hammer that refines our being, the earth is the anvil which is good for its time and purpose, and the world is the flame, for it seeks to try all. Some hardened shall shatter under the strike of a hammer, some shall be left with impurities because the flame was weak, but some shall be folded, twisted, hardened, hardened some more, worked many times over, removed of their impurities, and tempered, and they shall retain their strength, first from their Creator and again from their Savior. So be that which is tried and true and made straight again by way of the Lord before you leave the anvil.

God Himself is forging our faith, but even God needs His soldiers to put on the armor of life and fight for Him. He will set His holy armor upon us to protect us from the evil that is loosed in this world. We who believe in Him and fight for Him bear a sword of spirit, a shield of faith, a breastplate of righteousness, a belt of truth and feet of peace (Ephesians 6:10–17).

Folks, don't be that guy who, when asked, "What is God to you?" says, "He is my Lord and Savior," and end the conversation right then and there. Be that guy who, when asked, "What is Jesus to you?" says, "Where would you like me to begin?" A man who has not answers heaped up upon answers has a blind faith or a youthful faith (1 Peter 3:15). Even if he has wrong answers by interpretation, at least he tried, and a wiser man can help him, and I know not how far that will take a man, but I know this: that a man who dedicates time to learn about his Lord and Savior will surely be saved by Him.

A Puzzle for the Doctrines of Men

If you don't believe in Jesus being God in the flesh, I would like one last opportunity to try to convince you He is. The Torah says we are created in God's image and after His likeness. (Genesis 1:26–27) Imagine that, for a second, our God made us in His image after His likeness. So we were eternal and built similar to God. So God must be like our original state. I know I will die the first death as the law of sin and death demands, but I am still in the likeness of my God. I have a word that comes from my heart, and I have a mind which my spirit and heart reasons from, and I have a body of flesh. So if God is the Word in the beginning (John 1:1–2, Genesis 1:3) God spoke His will from His heart and the Spirit of God was also in the beginning to reason truth (Genesis 1:2; John 16:13) then who, what, when, where, why and how is His body? You better think long and hard about this question. Jesus Christ said on the cross forgive them for they know not what they do. (Maybe that was a reference to whom they do it to) (Luke 23:34) That is an great act of compassion. Who is better to die for your sin in the flesh then God Himself? I know of no great men but God Himself to be great. (John: 30–38) Seek the body of God. Genesis 1:1–3 For the God I served be made of a Word of, Spirit of, and Flesh of; this is thee embodiment of my God and only He is great, righteous and true.

And so I close this book with one final perplexing of your thoughts; what does this verse say in your heart:

> For I say unto you, That except your righteousness shall exceed the righteousness of the scribes and the Pharisees, ye shall in no case enter into the kingdom of heaven. (Matthew 5:20)

Brothers and sisters, see, listen, act, and love. Make the call today to the one truth that will hear, lest we become the heirs of our own destruction (The perpetuation of our political instructions January 27, 1838 Abraham Lincoln).

Go in peace to love and serve the Lord. Amen

About the Author

I have pretty much been a farmer from birth, and if you ever get a chance, start small and work your way up. I did the opposite and it was met with heavy resistance. I definitely have had a truly humbling life. The hard lifestyle of not having much, being on a farm, and learning things the hard way has really opened my eyes from a young age. I think the Buddha had it right on the fourth day when he ventured out; even with all the aging, sickness, death, we are all beggars, and we have to come to terms with that. The true joy, as spoken of in Ecclesiastes, can finally put our days in peace. My rage and anger stemmed from a lack of understanding. Even now, I can barely understand God's plan for me, but this I know: that when my fuse is lit, I know now to pull it from the charge, because God's plan has its own course. You and I can either go with the grain or against it. The old me is laughing at and provoking me to blow, but the new me has patience, because God, to me, is observable, testable, and He always replicates His results.

I truly did believe in God almost my whole life, even though we have had differences in how the plan is to be carried out. I am glad He never has left me. Jesus Christ, on the other hand, was extremely difficult for me to come to terms with. I guess that's what made Him so powerful in winning me over; He made me choose. No option C. I have been studying the Bible and doctrines now for about five years, and this is my first doctrine of hopefully many more to come.

My writing teacher once held me up after class after he read us a short story and made us make up the remainder of that story, and he told me this. "You have a very interesting mind, and you made up a pretty good story. I hope you keep writing." This gentleman has since passed away, but after writing this book, I see what he meant. I hope you have enjoyed this book.

CPSIA information can be obtained
at www.ICGtesting.com
Printed in the USA
BVHW041731180623
666060BV00005B/1282